ESSAYS FROM THE AIR

ESSAYS
FROM THE AIR

by

GEOFFREY GRIGSON

LONDON

ROUTLEDGE & KEGAN PAUL

First published 1951
by Routledge and Kegan Paul Ltd.
*68 Carter Lane, London, E.C.*4
and printed in Great Britain
by T. and A. Constable Ltd., Edinburgh

To J. P.-H., who first placed me
in the padded cells
of Whiteladies Road

INTRODUCTION

THESE TALKS were delivered over several years in various services of the B.B.C. Few of them are printed exactly as they were delivered, since the speaker in the studio departs even from his script in ways which would be intolerable in print. Perhaps he shouldn't, but he does. Now and again something which had to be cut for exigencies of time or speech has been restored. In a few of the talks a paragraph or two has been added for clearer illustration of the subject. Writers might disagree about the value to them of broadcasting, except as a means of publication. Too much obedience to the injunction 'Be natural' or to the warning 'But you would not *say* that' may make them write slackly and with too much repetition. These are arguments I must avoid, except to hazard that the naturalism of the broadcast talk is overdone and does not make for precision. My business is more to thank the B.B.C. and many talks producers, past and present, London and Regional, for the opportunity of broadcasting talks of the kind which I enjoyed preparing, for patience and good advice and much kindness over many years. Also, to thank correspondents from all over the country and from other countries who have written to me after the talks were given. It is their appreciation which has encouraged me to make a selection from many talks about many subjects. The selection is a miscellany, but whether the topic is grave-worms or the look of the West of England from a plane, the pleasures of jewellery or the features of William Wordsworth, the miscellany is tied together, I hope, by a unity of attitude and by a curiosity I trust not to be entirely that of the Jackdaw of Rheims.

GEOFFREY GRIGSON

9

CONTENTS

Introduction   *page* 9

1. The Invisible Worm   13

2. The Natural Order   20

3. The Pleasures of Jewellery   28

4. Jonathan Couch of Polperro   32

5. Skellig Michael   37

6. Culbone and 'Kubla Khan'   45

7. Paddington Station   51

8. Durham Cathedral   56

9. A Window in the Air   61

10. Edward Goddard, Gardener and Antiquary   66

11. Sir Joshua Reynolds   71

12. John Constable   78

13. Turner   83

14. Ruskin's 'Modern Painters'   88

15. Alfred Stevens and the Cat   95

16. How to Look at an Art Gallery   101

17. The Musée Wiertz, or the Uses of Bad Art   106

18. Squabbles about Art   112

19. Art for Everyone   116

20. English Novels   120

21. 'Moonfleet' and John Meade Falkner   125

CONTENTS

22. COBBETT IN WILTSHIRE   *page* 133

23. WORDSWORTH, NATURE, AND THE LAKES   138

24. THE LOOK OF WORDSWORTH   144

25. THE RHYTHMS OF POETRY   151

26. THE LANGUAGE OF POETRY   160

27. THE ENJOYMENT OF POETRY   171

28. THE MAKING OF A POEM   178

29. THOMAS CHATTERTON   186

I

THE INVISIBLE WORM

HOWEVER EXACTLY we know them, I suppose there are some truths we are never going to allow in daily usage. The sun does not rise or set, but nothing is going to expel 'sunrise' or 'sunset' from our vocabularies. It is not so very different with my invisible worm, the worm of graves, whose meat we become, or are supposed to become, but whose existence, if you think twice, is not demanded by common sense. The sun, after all, appears to rise, appears to set. But who has ever seen a grave-worm? Long ago in 1685 the sceptical Sir Thomas Browne wrote *Urn-Buriall*. There were advantages in being burnt. 'Urnal interments and burnt relicks lie not in fear of worms, or to be an heritage for serpents,' Sir Thomas declared; and then checked himself: 'In carnal sepulture, corruptions seem peculiar unto parts; and some speak of snakes out of the spinal-marrow'—a recollection of Pliny's *Natural History*—'but while we may suppose common worms in graves, it is not easy to find any there.' Not even the common earthworm. The curious doctor had investigated graves in Norfolk and found few earthworms, let alone worms generated within the body: 'Few in churchyards above a foot deep, fewer or none in churches, though in fresh decayed bodies.' I told someone lately, a sensible someone, well educated, whose father, like Sir Thomas Browne, is a doctor, how I had just seen that tomb of an early sixteenth century abbot in the abbey church at Tewkesbury. Stone worms, I said, wreathed about on his stone cadaver, though grave-worms did not exist. 'Nonsense,' she said. 'But they don't exist.' 'Of course they exist.' I have always found that friend of mine an obstinate champion of fallacies of common belief; and what she believes vaguely, yet firmly, most of us also go on believing. Grave-wormers are commoner than Flat-landers. So I have been digging—not in the same way as Sir Thomas Browne—for the invisible worm. He has to do with death, a subject, after all, our race has believed to be of some importance.

13

Timor mortis conturbat me; and one of the reasons why fear of death plunged me into a sixteenth century conturbation was what I supposed would happen to me—to my mere body—after my sixteenth century death.   There are never times when we think neither about death nor about life; but the emphasis does alter from one to the other, and becomes obvious in our symbolism. At the end of the thirteenth century, say, when they carved the fresh buttercups and hawthorn in the chapter-house of South-well Minster, life predominates.   But there came a change through the later Middle Ages in Northern Europe, a fixation of moral thought upon death and punishment, coupled in art, in monumental sculpture, in poetry, in sermons, with a realistic portrayal of the horrors of death.   It is clear in the *Summa Predicantium* of John Bromyard, the Chancellor of Cambridge University at the end of the fourteenth century.   In his sermon on the fate of the dead he catalogues the sins of the evil lovers of the world and when the end of everything comes 'instead of a great retinue and throng of followers, their body shall have a throng of worms and their soul a throng of demons'.   After another hundred years, morbidity about death becomes acute: the worm has his triumph, and so worms wriggle around the stony corpse which Abbot Wakeman ordered for himself at Tewkesbury, one such monument out of hundreds.

All the same, Abbot Wakeman is not a fair example for the Tudors.   He is a cleric.   He inherits the deathly and naturalistic moralism of John Bromyard; and in Tudor times death and the worm become allied contestants in a conflict as old as religion, and yet sharp in a new way.   Here are the Middle Ages against the Renaissance, here is religion against the exaggerated delight in the self-dependence of man, in the life and activities and lusts of this world, this here and now.   So *Timor mortis conturbat me* because I am haunted by the old world in the new.   I am anxious in my ambivalence; and I begin to fear death the terminator even more than the hell which may follow my death.   If I am a Tudor poet—even a Jacobean poet—the worms at my decaying corpse are the antithesis to my brave delights.   The fair body I enjoy may to-morrow be blotched with the plague, or turn damp and feverish with the Sweating Sickness.   I am clothed in silk. To-morrow I shall be clothed in corruption.   So the sixteenth century, with an overlap into the seventeenth, appears from one side among the wormiest and deathliest of periods, however energetic and courageous and lyrical it may be from the other. If there is much of love with naked foot stalking in my chamber, death in the Tudor age is always pushing a bald face through the petals or through the curtains of the bed.

Think of one of the commonplaces of Tudor poetry. About 1500 Skelton wrote a deathly poem in which the worms occur and 'dust' rhymes with 'lust' and with that short word of ineluctable compulsion, 'must'. Beauty and worms are joined by the nexus of vanity. Midway between Skelton and John Donne there is a poem in *Tottel's Miscellany* about dust and lust and worms and Helen of Troy:

> Where is become that wight
> For whose sake Troye town
> Withstood the Greeks till ten years' fight
> Had razed their walls adown?
>
> Did not the worms consume
> Her carrion to the dust?
> Did dreadful death forbear his fume
> For beauty, pride or lust?

Thomas Nashe was then a small boy. He grows up, the plague full swift goes by and he writes:

> Brightness falls from the air,
> Queens have died young and fair,
> Dust hath closed Helen's eye,
> I am sick, I must die.

And the worms are not missing, as in Nashe's prose of 1594: 'In the marrow of your bones snakes shall breed. Your mome-like crystal countenances, shall be netted over, and (masker-like) cawle-visarded, with crawling, venomous worms. Your orient teeth, toads shall steal into their heads for pearl; of the jelly of your decayed eyes, shall they engender their young.' And with the other hand Nashe writes with Renaissance gaiety of young lovers.

It would not be in the least difficult to make a vermicular anthology, a florilegium of Tudor and Jacobean worms, coming down to Shakespeare, Dekker, Tourneur, and Webster, that last inebriate of death. The murdered Clerk Saunders told the May Margaret in the ballad that he slept among the hungry worms. There are worms in hundreds of epitaphs in parish churches. I stared at one in the church I went to as a child:

> O what a nest of worms,
> A lump of pallid earth
> Is mud-walled man.
> Before we mount on high,
> We cope with change,
> We wander, alter, die.

It was on the memorial of a man who ventured his money in enterprises of the New World, which he may have visited himself in one of the ships out of Plymouth.

In the top drawer how fine a surfeit there is of Shakespearian worms—the Hamlet worms, or rather the Hamlet worm—'my Lady Worm' who owns the skull the grave-digger throws up; Mercutio turned into worm's meat; Henry VIII's Queen Katherine hoping the King will flourish 'When I shall dwell with worms'; Richard II proposing talk of 'graves, of worms, and epitaphs', making dust our paper and writing sorrow on the bosom of the earth; Rosalind, the Duke's daughter, remarking that 'Men have died from time to time and worms have eaten them, but not for love.' The complex of associations is mostly the same. The worms are in the mouth of kings or queens, dukes or duchesses; or they are soon going to be.

'Though we are eaten up of lice and worms,' says Bosola in *The Duchess of Malfi*,

> And though continually we bear about us
> A rotten and dead body, we delight
> To hide it in rich tissue.

And when the Duchess asks what she is, he replies savagely: 'Thou art a box of worm-seed, at best but a salvatory of green mummy.'

The invisible worm is indispensable under Queen Elizabeth, even under James I, but though so many of us still believe, or do not trouble to disbelieve, in his existence, he was getting near the end of his meat. He has ahead of him romantic moments of a highly morbid return, but being—for reasons which will soon be obvious—not quite so real, he can be degraded at last into a joke. If you made a jest about the worm in Tudor literature, it was a wry jest or a defiant one, with the worms waiting for you. But obviously the degradation had begun by the time you reach Marvell's vermicular joke in the poem 'To His Coy Mistress', published in 1681, three years after his death:

> Thy beauty shall no more be found;
> Nor, in thy marble vault, shall sound
> My echoing song: then worms shall try
> That long preserv'd virginity:
> And your quaint honour turn to dust,
> And into ashes all my lust.

The old associative words and rhymes, as you had them nearly two centuries before in Skelton, but these new worms are joke worms, more or less. And no wonder. Things have changed. The Royal Society has been formed, the virtuoso is about putting his nose into everything. The times are sceptical and inquisitive, and twenty-three years have passed since Sir Thomas Browne had been poking around Tombland in Norwich and announcing that we may suppose merely common worms in graves.

If the sixteenth century and its writers in book and church epitaph finally established and strengthened the worm at least as a property in our minds, the creature had a respectable antiquity. In the Bible, Job was conscious of the worm; the Authorized Version possesses the Tudor tang: 'If I wait, the grave is mine house: I have made my bed in the darkness. I have said to corruption, Thou art my father: to the worm, Thou art my mother and my sister.' Moreover, it is easy to understand how the concept of the grave-worm came about. Earthworms are universal, bodies are buried in the earth, and there they are out of sight, if not out of mind. Worm-like maggots appear in decaying flesh that is not buried. The only book in which I have seen a separate species of grave-worm invented and named happens to be a modern American novel about werewolves. But what made the worm so easy to accept without question or without bothering to be precise about the species was the ancient idea of 'spontaneous generation' or 'equivocal generation'. You, your dead body, bred the worms. That was the point. You were a box of worm-seed. The worm would be at you although you were lapped in lead. Worms within the lead would create no difficulty so long as spontaneous generation was accepted; and the acceptance is obvious in several of the pieces I have quoted.

The belief goes back beyond Pliny to Aristotle. Samson's dead lion producing bees which yield honey (you still see it on treacle tins) had produced them by spontaneous generation. Decaying flesh was believed to engender locusts, grasshoppers, butterflies and a good deal else; as well as worms. It was just after the Tudor triumph of the worm that spontaneous generation began to be assaulted, tested, and ridiculed. You will find good accounts of it and of the arguments against it in writers of the late seventeenth century, such as Derham and John Ray. In the absence of close observation, they point out, the idea had been convenient. There were maggots in cheese. Very well, they were spontaneously generated by the cheese. The grubby who did not wash had lice. The lice were generated from their sweat. Eels appeared in ponds from which there was no stream: they were generated spontaneously from the mud. Toads, so it was said, were found in rocks. Allow spontaneous generation and the explanation was simple; with the biblical and classical authority behind it.

Spontaneous generation was combated with *ex ovo omnia*, or *omne vivum e vivo*, all living things come from the egg, all life comes from life; and by the experiments of Francisco Redi, and Swammerdam, and Leeuwenhoek, and Malpighi, and the scientists of the Royal Society. Francisco Redi in 1668 had shown that no maggots appeared in meat if the flies were screened off by wire. So when the Rev. William Derham, F.R.S., published his *Physico-Theology* in 1713 he could pronounce: 'Spontaneous generation is a doctrine so generally exploded, that I shall not undertake the disproof of it'; which was vermicide to the worm, however much we have kept him sentimentally and conveniently and traditionally alive.

If the invisible worm could be convincingly resuscitated outside of casual belief and serio-comic songs (as in 'Ilkley Moor baht 'at', in which the worms will eat thee up and the ducks will eat the worms, and we shall eat the ducks), or if the worm had kept a brisker vitality, you might find him more often in the poetry of our own time, which is a deathly time, though one with discreet, hygienic, evasive differences. You might have found him in Mr. Eliot's poems, related as they are to Webster and the Elizabethans. Here and there, indeed, the invisible worm does wriggle about, for instance in the more sensational verse of Mr. Dylan Thomas, among other old properties, much as it had wriggled in the writing of Monk Lewis or in the mediaevalism of Swinburne. But Mr. Eliot, as a man of his own age, has preferred the Tarot pack, the rat by the gasworks, Mr. Klipstein and Mr. Krumpacker, the area basement and the unlit urban stairway. A rather refined taste has seen to it that our death symbol, as in painting from Paul Nash to Graham Sutherland and nearer still, has so often been the dead tree—nothing more human. Dead trees and not dead soldiers were Nash's symbols for the new world we created in the trenches. How different are Paul Nash and Thomas Nashe! The neo-Georgian hauntings have been more squeamish than the hauntings of the Tudor mind.

You may have guessed that I borrowed 'The Invisible Worm' from the poem by William Blake. It was cheating, because Blake's worm was one which flew in the night in the howling storm to destroy the crimson rose with his dark secret love. Yet I rather fancied that for all destructive worms of literature and symbolism, Benjamin Britten's setting of Blake's invisible worm might do as a perfect conclusion. I am not so sure. Remember the accepted reality of the worm, the reality of death. Also the accepted reality of resurrection, from the corrupt the incorruptible. No, the musical illustration is the defeat of death. Donne in his sonnet beginning 'Death, be not proud' and ending 'Death, thou shalt die' marks a Jacobean difference, rejects the morbid sensationalism of decay and worms and makes death again the instrument of immortality. You should hear it—the record is obtainable—set by Benjamin Britten, and sung by Peter Pears— a triumph over death, a better disinfectant of morbidity perhaps than science ridiculing spontaneous generation.

Third Programme, 1950

2

THE NATURAL ORDER

(This was less a 'talk' than an experiment in composed writing, to be read coolly into the microphone without the interference of the speaker's vocal personality.)

IN THE EVENING I brought home a bunch of Shepherd's Rod, the small and rather uncommon kind of teasel. I put the teasels in a jug and carried them up to my room, and was reading there after midnight. Then I looked up and saw a grey moth with dark brown eyes walking over one of the flowerheads. I watched it through a lens. As though it had lost its strength, it walked across the rounded flowers slowly. It was feeding. A brown elastic tongue bent down at a blunt right angle and felt into the flowers. The moth stayed five minutes on one flower-head. Then it walked down over the prickles of the stem, crossed to the stem alongside, and walked slowly again up to another flowerhead.

For two days my windows had been shut because of the rain, so for two days or more the moth had been shut in the room without food. Its wings were a little broken, a little tarnished from flying around the light. In the black outside the window-panes other moths were rapidly walking up and walking down the glass trying to get into the electric bulb, the sun, or the electric flower, in this deceptive enclosure.

My moth on the Shepherd's Rod was pathetic. These moths outside were malignant. The two eyes of each one glittered. It was difficult to stop watching them. Moths are evil and power in some of the paintings of the Anglo-Swiss artist Fuseli (who was a member of the Aurelian Society). Sometimes he created small demons in the shape of pallid insects, with their antennae quivering, their eyes glittering.

A moth with scarlet legs was now moving up and down the black glass in a fury, not walking but beating up and down with its wings. The moth on the Shepherd's Rod spoke of happiness and relief.

.   .   .   .   .

I have an Aeolian harp, which I forget all about for months. It lies in a corner, dust collects on the sound-box and cobwebs go across the strings. In the very hot weather a Canadian friend, who is writing about Coleridge, came down for the night. We took the harp out and wiped off the cobwebs and tightened the slack strings. A warm east wind seemed gusty and strong enough, so we tried the harp in the window downstairs. The direction of the wind was wrong. I took it up to a bedroom window and fastened it in a casement, and at once the music began to rise and fall. The wind which quivered the strings and brought the sound into the room, brought in as well a scent out of the heated garden. I had placed the harp, without thought of doing so, directly over a large jasmine trained on the wall below. So I had exactly recalled a moment out of the seventeen-nineties. Casement, harp, jasmine, night, a warm wind. It was a curious accident. A recreation of Coleridge's house at Clevedon, with the harp, the jasmine, and Sarah Fricker, that woman who plagued him as his wife, and of Coleridge's feelings which he described as 'all too delicate for use'.

.   .   .   .   .

My friend told me that years later Coleridge put down a note about himself and Doctor Johnson. Johnson's conversation was a repetition of the same notes on a big drum: his own was the vanishing music of an Aeolian harp. Johnson's drum notes would be remembered, his own weaving of Aeolian sounds would be forgotten. But Coleridge was wrong; at least about himself.

.   .   .   .   .

It was dark when I came back after fetching the Shepherd's Rod. It lives in a peculiar place. An inland cliff runs along through the country. At one point it juts over the plain and becomes a headland, narrow and abrupt. On this headland rise the low earthworks of a Norman castle; not one of the permanent castles of stone, but rather a fort of earthen banks topped with

palisading. I have known the place for a long while, but for the
first time I saw how it was. Cattle had trodden down the vegeta-
tion. First the headland was cut from the upper plain by a
ditch and a long high bank. Within the bank, rectangular shapes
of buildings were visible on the level ground of the basecourt.
Here and there the ground descended into deep pits, and the pits
were filled with nettles as though organic rubbish had been tipped
into them long ago, giving the nettles nitrogen for their growth.
Then, as one came towards the point of the headland, one crossed
a second ditch, much deeper than the first and circling a tall
mound of earth, before the headland fell sharply through trees
to the lower plain. This was the *motte*, on which the wooden
tower of the castle had been raised so that the soldiers could look
across the world behind and below.

I searched around in the rabbit holes and found one delicate
sherd of a Norman pitcher.

.   .   .   .   .

How right that this castellated headland should also nourish
a number of rare or at least uncommon plants! The Shepherd's
Rod grows in the tangles below. It does not spread much, but
this year it has jumped fifty feet up the cliff. Some trees had
been felled. The slope had been emptied, and then had been
scored by the pulling out of the trunks. The seeds had come
up to this bare ground and grown into a thicket of plants.
Probably other species will be too strong, and the tenancy of the
Shepherd's Rod will last only a year or two. It will continue only
in the ancient colony further down.

I had never found another plant of the headland, a tall ever-
lasting pea. I knew about it, and now the castle discovered it
for me. It was there, climbing into the nut bushes when I slid
from the mound into the outer ditch. Both these plants have
been quietly growing here, never much increasing, never much
diminishing, for at least sixty years. Botanists long ago dead
have come to see them. They may have been growing here when
the castle was built. They are linked to the castle, but the link
has nothing to do with men. It is geological, not human. The
accident of geology gave the acquisitive and severe Normans a
place admirable for observation and for defence, it gave these

plants the one place in all the miles around where they could endure. I was happy coming home in the dark with my two plants and my one sherd of Norman pottery.

Another accident: had the cliff not been made of chalk, which crumbles onto the plain, had there been springs of water, a stone castle might have followed the castle of wood, a town would have assembled under the walls, a cathedral might have risen up. All the character of our lives around here would now be different.

· · · · ·

It is a good thing to keep a lens in one's pocket. Using the eyes always at the same focus conceals too much, it takes away from us the variety of enjoyment. So good writing depends on this shifting of focus, on its lengthening and shortening. Working downstairs very late, when the others of the household were asleep, I was slightly aware several times of a rustling on the floor, among some newspapers. After it had become irritating, I put my hand down to find the cause. A long slug was moving among the sheets. I picked up the paper, and looked at the slug under the lens. How curious a world of creatures I saw! I knew nothing of the life or morphology of slugs, but over the long slime of this black monstrosity very small white creatures were hurrying as though on skates. Near the head there were holes into the slug on either side, which I discovered since are the orifices into the lung. These orifices were opening and shutting, rhythmically. The white creatures were skating with no effort into the orifice and out. In they went: the orifice closed gently. It opened as gently: out they came.

The slug was an ice-rink, or the long black canal of a Dutch painting.

I felt like the Dutchman Leeuwenhoek watching the wriggling of spermatozoa through his microscope for the first time in human history, a Columbus peering into a New World.

· · · · ·

In the volume I have on Leeuwenhoek a peculiar footnote is appended to this discovery, that 'it was announced in a letter written to the Royal Society in November 1677—at the very moment when the marriage of William and Mary was being celebrated in London'.

. . . . .

Or mosquitoes. We were interested to identify the mosquitoes which were being a nuisance around the house. They are not difficult to catch and kill without injuring their delicate structure. Stalk them with a glass. Hold a cigarette in the left hand, a glass in the right. Invert the glass over the mosquito on the wall, pull at the cigarette, and raise the glass very slightly and blow in the smoke. Soon the mosquito swoons to the side of the glass. It is better, though, to examine them alive than asphyxiated. Alive and tense. Each an instrument of precision, hairless and elegant, exquisite in the lines.

Direct the lens onto a gnat: an angry, insignificant, self-important, shapeless dot of hairiness.

. . . . .

The natural order is regarded as indecent and common by English intellectuals at the moment. The superficial reason may be only accidental and transitory. A deeper reason is that we are English, and though we like nature, we do not love it, or fear makes us love it only in select parcels. We do not love it totally. We think nature has been found out. We are like Ruskin, shocked to learn of plants which devour insects and complaining of the 'nasty things' in nature who no longer deserved so many of his compliments. I wonder, then, how we take that early book by André Gide, *Les Nourritures Terrestres*, which has lately been translated with the English title of *The Fruits of the Earth*?

Do not intellectuals, and others, realize we have to exist on the earth? We may as well enjoy what it has to give, which is a great deal, and delightful too, as Gide proclaimed, and we may as well enjoy it as long as each of us has the capacity, without being afraid, without making exceptions.

It is true Gide's natural history is universal. It includes water coming to birth under black rocks, light, figs, waves, the falling of yellow leaves, forms, thoughts, and a philosophy and all human appetites—yes, all. It does not push men out of the natural paradisiacal order with the flaming sword of that archangel who for all his glory was christened over a low church font and flogged into learning by a clerical headmaster.

No, certainly, it is not a book an Englishman could have managed, since the time of the extraversion of our interest onto nature. Lawrence is a candidate. He was too dotty. Hopkins is another. The archangel had him in a different way. Patmore, had greater intelligence been given him, might have come nearest; but nearest is nowhere near at all.

If we enjoy too much, we are off towards mysticism and pantheism. We are not balanced. We do not like form. We do not allow ourselves full enjoyment. We have to justify even our select enjoyment; and we often make a good thing of the process. Or else self-excluded, we narrow the selection still more and emasculate nature into a sentiment, a pin-up.

Gide is an archangel himself. We should add, he is a fallen angel; and a foreign one.

·   ·   ·   ·   ·

A very simple thing can be felt, but not known and so not felt completely. Very much aloft in Grand Canary, a slope moved up and stopped at the cloudless sky. Out of it grew immensely tall stems of fennel supporting yellow umbels. Turning the other way, the island fell to an illimitable Atlantic of clouds over the real Atlantic.

I was struck with the tallness of the fennel, and I remembered the stalks and the flowers in union with everything else. To-day I find in Gide's book (he was in Africa): 'The huge stalks of fennel (a blaze of green and gold in the golden sunlight or under the azure-tinted leaves in the motionless eucalyptus) shone with incomparable splendour that morning of early summer on our road through the Sahel.

Were the eucalyptus trees astounded or placid?'

Exactly: and at last I knew and felt, and felt more entirely, the stalks and flowers of the fennel on the summit of the Canaries.

Gide was not afraid. More than that he was *all there*. He did not mutilate the natural order. He shortened and lengthened the focus of his eye, his intention, and his thought.

·   ·   ·   ·   ·

Sometimes I bring back as a memento a part of something I have seen in the happiest conditions of mind, and light, and neighbourhood. Now and then it has been a plant or seeds which would develop into plants. It does not always work. The plant may flourish, but may insist, properly, on becoming itself in a new neighbourhood. Or it may insist on calling up something pointless or irritating to remember out of the circumstances around that moment when I first looked at it wholeheartedly.

A burr-marigold. It has the smallest of golden flowerheads and a black stem, the black entering into the green of the foliage. I collected the seeds in the garden of a hotel in the Canaries. It should recall itself as I saw it first, the light, the equable heat, the total exultation, the water from the hose spreading and darkening the soil under the oleanders and the angel's trumpets, and the noise of sucking which emerged quietly from the darkened soil. It does not. It recalls—now why?—the vacancy of a schnapps-taking Northerner alongside of whom I had taken a glass of Los Lirios just before: his vacancy, his previous conversation, and the sweat on his nose above his spectacles, and the untidy, unfaced concrete of the hotel which they were building and of which only the first floor and the bar and the dining-room were finished. Yet the Los Lirios tasted and smelt most deliciously. I am too weak or else the plant is not strong enough.

· · · · ·

Associations are the devil, perhaps another disease of English writers, and useless if they are not of the highest, or a high order of relevance. The only reapers they know in Canada are large combine-harvesters. My Canadian friend told me of a woman who taught in a Canadian school. When she came—whenever she came—to Wordsworth's 'Solitary Reaper', single in the field, she could not rid herself of a combine-harvester, single in the twilight of a Canadian prairie. (Or did I take it wrongly, did she know the poem only by name and believe it to be a poem about a combine-harvester?)

Still, a good association can drive out one which is less good, less relevant. My Shepherd's Rod from now on will not have so much to do with the Norman citadel and basecourt, but more

(I hope) to do with the starved moth finding nectar and comfort in the white flowers; and so more to do with happiness.

. . . . .

But we shall see. It may bring back the malignancy of the moth outside the window, and the scarlet legs and the eyes of the small devil. Alas, the longer we live, the more we feel and know, the more evident it becomes, even now in our time, that happiness and not fear or doubt, let alone malignancy, is the condition in which the great things are contrived. The preaching artist has too much impurity. He has doubts, he has something to conceal, like Ruskin, or like some of the converted Catholic writers of England at the present time. I do not need to quote the texts or to mention examples. The great things proclaim it, the lives and remarks of the contrivers repeat it behind the picture, the book, the building, and the music. Sadly, it takes many of us too long to detect, and then to admit, this platitude.

Third Programme, 1950

3

THE PLEASURES OF JEWELLERY

SEVERAL OF US were having lunch together and were planning a book about gold. The metal, real gold, including gold money you could have in your purse or in your pocket. We complained about how few precious objects we have to-day in our lives and on our persons. We pay by paper, by postal orders, by cheques, and by grubby pound notes. Then, I saw an object on the cloth, and it was gold. A gold coin, a Celtic gold stater with a horse on it, which one of us had taken from his waistcoat and laid on the white table-cloth. He said it had been discovered in digging the foundations of a factory in Northern Germany, but it might have been minted that morning. I picked it up, I let it lie in the hollow of my hand, thick, heavy, quite remarkably soft; and, above all, precious.

There is much to be said in the days of the substitute and of plastics for indulging a delight in precious objects and indeed for haunting the commonest galleries of a minor art—the art of the making of jewellery. Here and there (and now and then, since you must not run a personal pleasure to death) I get much reward from putting my face close to the glass of jewellers' shops and seeing what the jeweller has in his second-hand tray. Alongside, new and neatly stuck into mauve beds of imitation velvet, he will have his modern stock—jewellery of the kind in which the settings are jazz-modern and the gems (if they are real ones) are jazz-cut, and the family of gems, the diamonds, the sapphires, the rubies, the emeralds, the topaz, amethyst, garnet, alexandrite, and so on, are made to quarrel and swear at each other. In this I am a reactionary of the years of B.C., or Before Cubism; and it is to the second-hand tray that my eye goes with relief. Brooches, rings, earrings, bracelets, English, French, Bohemian, Oriental, not very ancient, not even very valuable or expensive, yet contrived from precious metals and stones, though small ones, by lapidaries who did not know so much as to-day's craftsmen about the cutting of gem stones, but who did respect colour, relation, and design. It is extraordinary how much there is to choose from and enjoy. About a hundred years ago, I suppose, we ceased making the finer objects which become antiques with the advance of time. But there are more rings than there are grandfather clocks by Tompion, or by the clock-maker of the country town. Every woman, after all, has had eight fingers; and if she has not worn rings upon all of them, she may have sparkled with more than one ring per ring finger and kept several others in her jewel-box. It does not put me off to think of all the hundreds of thousands of dead fingers, now dry bones, between Queen Anne and Queen Victoria, and so to remember how rings alone are more immensely abundant than any other kind of antique. And if you are content with good looks, the lesser rings are much less expensive than other antiques. Garnets from Bohemia among points of gold can look as well as the vast ruby of caliphs.

Precious means to me both wonderful and once-upon-a-time, words which fit in well with jewels. Once upon a time, then (according to Hakluyt's *Voyages*), Ivan the Terrible, Czar of Muscovy, beckoned an Englishman into his jewel room in the Kremlin, into which he was carried every day in his chair. He called for jewels and he spoke about their virtue, beginning with a unicorn's horn set with diamonds, rubies, sapphires, and emeralds. Diamonds, said Ivan, he never liked, because they restrained fury and luxury. He pointed to a ruby: 'Oh, this is the most comfortable to the heart, brain, vigour and memory of man.' And then to an emerald, which the Czar said possessed 'the nature of the rainbow and was an enemy to uncleanness'; next, to a sapphire which he delighted in greatly because 'it preserves and increases courage, joy, and vital senses, it is precious and very sovereign to the eye, and takes away blood shot'. Last, he took an onyx in his hand and pronounced: 'All these are God's wonderful gifts, secrets in nature, and yet he reveals them to man's use and contemplation, as friends to grace and virtue and enemies to vice.' Then the interview came to an end, and the Czar said, 'I faint, carry me away until another time.'

We inherit, perhaps none too clearly, a feeling like the Czar's about the wonder and the preciousness of gems. If we swallow no crushed amethysts and hang no emeralds about children's necks to ward off epilepsy (medicines not available under the Health Scheme), I do not think our attraction to gem stones is purely aesthetic. Precious stones are not used to make garden paths except in fairy tales. They are rare, they seem to mix light with colour, they seem alive, and if they are no longer curative or magical, they fascinate us legitimately as they fascinated the Sumerians six thousand years ago. They are a proper symbol of royalty. The possession of them or the contemplation of them imparts just so much richness and royalty to our poorer, commoner selves. I have felt this after buying for less than the cost of two pairs of blankets or the cost of a hen-house one of those regard-rings they made in the eighteenth century, on which *regard*, in gems, the nearest possible word to *love*, is spelt out with a Ruby for R, Emerald for E, Garnet for G, Amethyst for A, and then Ruby again for R, and Diamond for D. I am a gazer, though, rather than a collector; and I use my fancy for precious stones to illuminate dark moments, much as jewellers' shops illuminate the wettest, blackest, windiest cities in the industrial North. I have had delight out of such windows on wet early closing days in February in Sheffield or the sooty canyons of Bradford, eyeing lapis lazuli, amber, Whitby jet, garnets (which satisfy me as much as any stone), tortoiseshell brooches inlaid with flowers in gold or platinum, corals bedded in yellow gold, or those Victorian brooches which are filigreed with minute golden shot or golden pearls. There is a story by Leskov of a poor peasant woman in a mud house in Bohemia who took off her shoe to hit a blood-fattened, blood-coloured bed bug on the wall. It was no bug, but a garnet, which tumbled out onto the floor.

As gold and garnets are sometimes found together, I have thought of a week in the ancient gold-diggings of Ireland or the gold-fields they worked in the last century in the far north of Scotland—up to the knees in a trout stream with a miner's pan.

Substitutes and plastics—they are the unpardonable degradation of jewel stones proper to the age of the democratic mass, softening what should be hard, providing make-believe and vulgarizing the exceptional. Back this goes to the eighteenth century when the first methods were contrived of making or faking jewel stones out of glass. It is the habit of our world,

THE PLEASURES OF JEWELLERY

On the air I once heard an American song of indubitable and sad poetry which went like this:

> Love, O Love, O loveless Love
> Has set our hearts on goldless gold.
> > From milkless milk
> > And silkless silk
> We are growing used to soulless souls.
> Such grafting times we never saw,
> That's why we have a pure food law.
> In everything we find a flaw,
> Even Love, O Love, O loveless Love.

Hatefully true.   Still, pain can be said to increase pleasure, and for your delight and my delight there are all these jewellers' windows around England and around all of Europe; and any jeweller will teach you in five minutes how you distinguish gems from gemless gems.

Home Service, 1950

4

JONATHAN COUCH OF POLPERRO

WHEN I WAS a boy in Cornwall, I knew in Polperro two old Miss Couches. Dry ladies they seemed to a child, who had dry Christian names and wore high lace collars propped up at intervals with whalebone. They were the daughters, in his old age, of Jonathan Couch, country doctor and naturalist and grandfather of 'Q'—of Sir Arthur Quiller Couch. He kept a book which I have been able to read—'Memorials of the Family of Couch noted by Jonathan Couch', though really it was an intermittent journal. Towards the end, under September 11th, 1860, I found one of the old ladies I knew: 'Born our little daughter and registered with the name of Bertha.'

Old Jonathan Couch, an ichthyologist whose reputation is not dead and a Fellow of the Linnaean Society, was seventy-one when that child was born, and there were two more to follow. He had been doctor then in Polperro for half a century. The family into which he had been born in 1789 had been yeomen either in Talland or Lansallos, though his grandfather was in business at Polperro as a fish-curer. The family had slipped a little. His father was a fisherman, and one of the first, he claimed, in Polperro to use a seine instead of the old drift nets. He was an only child, and he describes his father and mother as 'people of good sense, but of little learning'; they were independent, and determined to give this only child a good education. So when he was eight and a half they sent him away to a boarding school. Away—only three miles away, but he felt the separation as though it had been in Northumberland. The school was kept by a John Milton in the neighbouring parish of Pelynt, but it was a better school than one would find nowadays in an isolated part of the country. There he began his Latin 'under the care', he says, 'of an emigrant Polish priest, who had escaped from the horrors of the French Revolution'; an individual, he notes with a dissenting stab, who used to go over to the mansion of Trelawne —'and thus it came to pass that Popery was introduced into the family of the Reverend Sir Harry Trelawny'. He remembered a great frost in the seventeen-nineties when he was still at this school, during which he saw 'a Salmon which was frozen so stiff as to be capable of standing on its end'. He went on to the Grammar School at Bodmin (the school in later years of Edward Calvert the artist, and friend of Blake and Samuel Palmer). 'About this date Buonaparte was beginning to render himself conspicuous in France . . . Companies of volunteers were form'd in all directions, and those who were not actually enroll'd, had some specific duty assigned them in case of Invasion: such as driving off cattle and goods, setting fire to Corn, etc. I remember some honest hearted Individuals who liv'd in continued fear, dreading to go to bed, lest they should wake up at the sound of the Trumpet, or in the midst of the French troops.' They expected a diversion into Cornwall while the main attack was aimed at London.

He says nothing about how he became a naturalist. He left school and was apprenticed to a doctor at Looe, joining the East and West Looe Volunteer Artillery as a second lieutenant, paying for his own uniform. 'And here let me record something which my family may congratulate themselves upon among many that perhaps may lift their heads much higher. Neither myself nor those of mine who have lived before me, have ever sought to evade those imposts laid on them by Government for the well-being of the State; nor have we sought to suck the vitals of the Country to reimburse ourselves. We have not retir'd from the scene when danger threaten'd; and gave our efforts with a free heart, without fee, tho' attended with loss; for my clothes and accoutrements cost very nearly twenty pounds.' Here and there he slips in a curious note about Polperro. On the first umbrella, for example, 'the first that was ever spread in Polperro', which was 'a present from a merchant of Guernsey, at a time when smuggling was carried on from that Island to a great extent to Mr. Charles Guy, who kept the Ship Inn at Polperro. It was I think of a Crimson Colour; and as it pass'd thro' the Street, all the people were seen gazing from the doors, uttering their comments on the Pride of the User.' Another thing he records (to illustrate, in his own words, 'the slow progress of improvement in times not long since past') was the appearance of a peculiar object on the beach. 'I have heard my father say that when he was a boy the spout of a tea kettle was wash'd ashore by the sea; and it puzzled everyone to think what it could be. The wisest among them thought it the bowl of some strange sort of tobacco pipe.' In his father's Polperro boyhood during the seventeen-fifties tea was expensive, and tea-drinking was an unknown luxury in the poverty of a fishing village cut off by high hills and bad roads.

For Dr. Couch it was, on the whole, an easy, placid, prosperous, uneventful nineteenth-century life which he lived in Polperro. He stirred himself—a very nineteenth-century thing to do—to discover the coat of arms of Couch, he sent papers to the learned societies which flourished in the Industrial Revolution of Cornwall, he studied fishes as they came in onto the quay, and marine creatures, he worked bit by bit on the big achievement of his life, his still useful *History of British Fishes*, he searched out the rarer plants of the neighbourhood in habitats where they are still growing, he received the naturalists who called on him; and in his old age he was elected a corresponding member of the Zoological Society. In June 1866 he stuck in the cutting from a newspaper which records the honour, surrounded it in red and blue and yellow and green water-colour and underlined his name in green.

One day in the 'fifties he had a picture painted of himself holding the tusk of a walrus; and on the same day, at Trelawne, the son-in-law of Sir Harry Trelawny took a 'Photograph Collodion likeness' of him, full length, holding, this time, a tusk of an African barbiroussa or wart-hog. Photography was young then. The print stuck into the Memorials has faded, but there he is, one elbow on the table supporting the tusk, wearing a frock-coat with a half-velvet collar. The face is knobbly, full, determined, the lower jaw large, a full mouth sticking out, and especially the lower lip—a face more full of personality than beauty and clearly belonging to 'Q's' grandfather, though it lacks 'Q's' air of a larger world outside Cornwall. He was a local man of many interests—botany, ornithology, ichthyology, entomology, folklore, though not gardening or antiquities. How, I wonder, did he take *The Origin of Species*, published in 1859 when he was seventy? Couch was a Methodist, a fundamentalist, too, I would guess, sharing the attitude to Darwinism of Philip Henry Gosse (whom he knew) which is described with such poignancy in *Father and Son*. He had his aesthetic limitations or cautions. Modernism in the shape of Tennyson came to see him. 'In 1848, June 20, I receiv'd a visit from Mr. Alfred Tennyson the Poet . . . He came to Polperro in a Boat . . . and after viewing our scenery in all directions and taking tea at our house, they all rowed back to Fowey late in the evening. I found him well inform'd, and communicative: I believe a good Greek Scholar, with some knowledge of Hebrew. His personal appearance is not prepossessing: having a slouch in his gait, and rather slovenly in his dress, tho' his clothes were new and good. He confesses to this. He admir'd the wildness of our Scenery, and deprecated the breaking in of improvements, as they are term'd. He enquir'd after traditions, especially of the great Arthur: his object in visiting the County being to collect materials for a Poem on that Chief. But he almost doubted his existence. He show'd me a MS. Sketch of a history of the Hero; but it was prolix and modern.'

So much for Tennyson. No one else of such eminence is mentioned in these Memorials, which contain little of the outside world, little of natural history, and much of Dr. Couch's wives, of whom there were three in the nineteenth-century manner. The last marriage, which led to the old Miss Couches, was in 1858, when the doctor was sixty-nine. The first was in 1810. 'Q' was descended from the marriage in between, to Jane Quiller in 1815. It is the first marriage (as one would expect) of which he wrote the most vivid, touching memorial. She—she was Jane Rundle—died in the year of her wedding after giving birth to a daughter. Folded up in the book are two sheets of paper in which, after her death, Jonathan Couch gave an account of his courtship. He went over to Looe in 1805 to fetch some vaccine from the Looe doctor and then saw her first when he was sixteen. 'Dr. Prynne ask'd me if I wanted a good wife that could make pies (which she was then doing).' They became engaged, and they married when he was twenty-one. He made her a pair of earrings which she wore to her death, and which he then removed to give to their daughter. They quarrelled during their engagement, and 'these earrings would have been return'd to me, but she could not get them from her ears'. He gave her a parasol when he went to London to finish his doctor's training, and she gave him a handkerchief with his initials worked in a corner in her own hair. The prematurely born child survived, but after his wife squeezed his hand for the last time and died, he wrote: 'Thus passes away the glory of the world.' Two years later, on the anniversary of her death, he wrote again: 'When I forget thee, my own dear Jane, may my right hand forget her cunning! Still I feel I love her and ever shall, but let me not again set up an Idol in my heart as I have done.' Fifty-six years later, after his third marriage, when he was seventy-seven, he wrote a poem, thinking of a lock of this girl's yellow hair which he had mislaid, beginning:

> Only one link—a link of gold—
> Between the past and me.

But he had his solace, if less in the second and third wives and their children, then in the gleaming fishes of which he made water-colours on the quay, in his plants, in his phenological records of Polperro which he kept year by year, in the pursuit of natural history which I suspect no wife, first, second, or third, ever shared. Naturalists have a habit, reprehensible, no doubt, of being married to their natural history, gardeners one of being married to their gardens. Both have a family of extra children who are never christened.

West of England, 1946

5

SKELLIG MICHAEL

IF YOU spread out the Ordnance Survey maps of Ireland, of the west coast from Donegal in the north to Kerry in the south, it is surprising how often you will see in Gothic letters the words Church or Oratory. You find these Gothic symbols of antiquity on Rathlin O'Byrne Island, Achill, Clare, Tory Island, the Blaskets, and now and than a saint's name will be added. If you cross to the islands, still perhaps in the greasy bottom of a curragh which glitters with mackerel scales, the humble ruins you find on the bare brown backs of these Atlantic islands survive from a remote Christianity, from that extraordinary flowering of devotion and meditation which began with the mission of St. Patrick.

Patrick came to Ireland in 432. He was trained, or so it appears, in an island monastery in the Mediterranean, and though he was sympathetic to monasticism, he did his main work in Ireland through bishops and secular clergy. Monasticism began there in his own century, but it was after his death (Patrick died in 461), in the sixth century and the seventh, that monasteries sprang up all over Ireland. It was in these centuries that so many of the Irish saints and monks felt the need to live more austerely, more purely, more by themselves on the immense shores and the unfriendly islands of the Atlantic. They went into the desert. They built themselves monasteries much smaller than those on the mainland or in the richer country. They made the west of Ireland into a Thebaid. Indeed the rule they lived by was that of the Egyptian monk, St. Pachomius, who was the founder of monasticism, of ordered meditation, in the deserts of Upper Egypt.

Of all the relics of this Christianity pushed to the last verge of the known world, the one I most wanted to visit, and have lately visited, was the monastery on Skellig Michael, more than eight miles out in the Atlantic, off the blackness of Kerry. I cannot pretend that I went there very well prepared. Accounts of Skellig

Michael or Great Skellig and of Little Skellig which lies alongside in the swell of the Atlantic, have to be searched for in libraries, and it was a search I had not made. My clue—enough certainly to drive me on—was botanical, not archaeological. In a guide to Irish plants I had read that the Skelligs were pinnacles of rock: 'Great Skellig', the account of a few lines went on, 'rises like a cathedral to 714 feet; a group of ruined beehive huts, the dwellings of early anchorites, clings to its precipitous slopes. The Little Skellig, also lofty, is the breeding place of thousands of gannets.' It was not accurate altogether, it gave a wrong picture, but it decided me to go, and it brought me past Killarney, and down through the Kerry mountains, and along Dingle Bay, and across the ferry to the village of Knights Town in Valencia Island. Knights Town, I reckoned, would be one of the nearest villages to Skellig Michael where we could hire a motor-boat. I knew a little of the difficulties of landing on islands, not to say pinnacles of rock, in the Atlantic, so as we went slowly across Ireland in the train, stopping at every station, I was wondering if the weather would last, and watching, a bit anxiously, to see how much the grass alongside was being bent over in the wind. Not much, though the wind freshened and the grasses became more agitated as the train crept along the side of the mountain above Dingle Bay. We were lucky. The wind remained gentle, and the sea quiet; and—at a price—it was not difficult to get a motor-boat for the day. I read later how in the 'nineties a large party of the Royal Society of Antiquaries in Ireland waited, with their wives, to see if they could cross to Skellig from Dingle. 'By courtesy of the Rear-Admiral Commanding' they were to be transported in H.M. Gunboat *Banterer*. The *Banterer* arrived through the mist. The lieutenant would take the learned men, but would not be responsible for the learned men's wives, who were left on the quay disappointed and protesting. The *Banterer* sailed out of the mist—into the sunshine and perfection of a quiet Atlantic.

Valencia lies within a great natural harbour circled with mountains, a good way in from the sea; and from Knights Town, at least, Skellig Michael was invisible. The journey from the pier would be about eighteen miles, nearly half of it down the fiord to the coast. This meant that Skellig would continue to be invisible until we crept out between Valencia Island and the mainland of Kerry. And at last we did so creep out of the fiord, from calm onto the mild heave of the Atlantic; and there, nine miles away, nine miles out from the immense black cliffs we were leaving, was Skellig Michael on the horizon. The sea was blue, the clouds behind Skellig Michael (and Little Skellig) were a pale dove colour. Skellig Michael shot up from its narrow base, but not as a perfect triangle since the high point was cut off by the clouds. Now and again, as we came nearer, the clouds shifted and the whole immense triangle of the island was clear. Little Skellig was far less regular in shape, and since it is a good many feet lower, was not capped with the clouds. Great Skellig changed slowly from blue to dark. Little Skellig, under its wildly fretted outline of Gothic pinnacles, appeared by contrast to be in the sunshine. After a while I suspected and then became certain that the sunshine was made up of all the ivory-white gannets crowding along the ledges. Little Skellig, so James Fisher tells me, is the third largest gannetry in the world. I could believe it when we were close enough to see the ledges and the gannets passing like snowflakes against the darkness of Skellig Michael, and when at last we entered the smell of guano, which extends away out to sea from the gannetry.

I must confess (and it is, and was then, a little disappointing) that as well as the relics of Celtic Christianity on Skellig Michael there exists a lighthouse, though on the side towards New York and the Statue of Liberty. It means that it is easier to land in fair weather, Trinity House having long ago contrived a quay and a minute harbour and blasted a path around the precipices. But it also means that the lower steps which climbed nearly six hundred feet, very sharply, from the landing-place to the beehive huts, were also blasted away. After you land nowadays, you walk prosaically for some two hundred yards along a narrow, well-contrived road, before you turn off and start to scale the island by another flight of steps.

After five hundred steps or so, there comes a point when you need—or when I needed—to rest. You do so at a spot called Christ's Saddle, and there you realize for the first time the configuration of Great Skellig. Resting on the cushions of sea-pink, just under the clouds which were veiling past, I could now see that Skellig Michael was not one acute triangle, but two, joined by the bare earth and rock of Christ's Saddle. Indeed from north and south of Bolus Head (which is the nearest point on the mainland) Great Skellig always appears as a twin-peaked mountain and not as the single, triangular peak it had been to us as we crossed from Valencia Island. We climbed again, the steps turning to the right up the lower peak. That botanical account prepared me for a number of beehive huts, in ruins, scattered here and there among the sea-pink and the scurvy-grass, and clinging, clinging as it said, to the precipices. I was not expecting

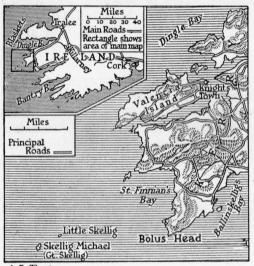

A. J. Thornton

these steps, I was not expecting the pavement we had now reached up above the Atlantic, or the high wall now pierced by more steps and a doorway, through which we entered into an enclosure. And inside the enclosure? Inside, like conical heaps of hay drying on an Irish field, there was a humpy row of *clochans*, or beehive huts. In ruins? Not a bit of it. They were more or less perfect. Nothing was ruinated except the small church of St. Michael, around which the huts were grouped on three sides. And if the huts were built in the eighth century or the seventh, the ruined church had obviously been a later mediaeval building.

At once I realized I had seen all this before, though less perfectly. I remembered the slope of another island, St. Helen's, a desert island, smaller and less steep, and thick with bracken and brambles, among the Isles of Scilly. Incendiaries from a German raider burnt this Scillonian island off during the war, and revealed a Celtic monastery on just such a plan as this. In the centre the ruins of a mediaeval church, around the church the foundations of one cell or hut after another, and all around them the foundations of another such wall enclosing the precincts or 'cashel' of the monastery. Only here on Skellig Michael all was more or less complete. The first large hut, perhaps the refectory, the common meeting-place, was perfect. Stones of white quartz let into the conical dry walling above the doorway were formed into a cross. We bent under the wide slate lintel, and went into the clean spacious interior. It was lit by window-holes above our heads, the floor was paved, pegs of slate stuck out from the walls. From these, perhaps, depended on thongs the leather 'book-cases', or satchels, in which the liturgical books were kept. A few such Irish satchels have survived. The use of them belonged to monasteries of the Pachomian Rule, and Curzon found satchels of the kind in one of the monasteries he visited in 1865 by the Natron Lakes in Egypt. He gives a picture of them hanging from pegs in the wall in his book on the monasteries of the Levant.

The Irish monasteries, and Skellig Michael, and no doubt the monastery on St. Helen's in the Isles of Scilly, followed, as I have said, the rule of St. Pachomius, so far away in Egypt, in most of the details of their arrangement and no doubt of their monastic life. Here, as St. Pachomius laid it down, was the surrounding wall, the refectory, the cells, the church, though perhaps the original church of Skellig Michael was the beehive oratory along-side the little ruined, roofless, mediaeval church. This beehive hut has an altar built into the eastern wall, and above the altar a slit-shaped window giving a view only of the sea. Beehive is accurate enough, but the word 'hut' does not justly describe the shape, character, or skilful design and well-laid masonry of these ancient *clochans*, which have survived, more or less intact, a thousand years of Atlantic exposure. A High Cross, roughly shaped and incised, sticks up and leans over to one side among the cells, like a totem pole in a primitive village. Just beyond it, raised up by a wall and stuck with smaller crosses, there is a minute and no doubt overcrowded graveyard. Built into the ground below the huts are two wells, small pools from which the monks drew their water and where also they washed as they were enjoined to do before eating.

It was extraordinary to be out and up on this rock, this maritime mountain, this Michael's Mount, where under the proper protection of St. Michael the Archangel, the Irish monks had reproduced the religious austerities of the Egyptian desert. Enough is known of Irish monasticism to be sure of how they lived their penitential life as a *militia Christi* on Skellig Michael. The details you can find in Father Ryan's *Irish Monasticism*. They watched and prayed and worked in self-mortification. They prayed before dawn by candlelight, and again at sunset, and after a little sleep again at midnight when they were woken up for the night vigil, the *nocturnae solemnitates*. The asceticism of labour was enjoined for them under the Pachomian Rule: they could neither talk nor laugh at work; rather they must pray, meditate, and chant the psalms. On Skellig Michael, on the precipitous slopes (which drop away to the Atlantic from the cashel walls), you might think there was little opportunity for the gardening and the corn-growing of Irish monasteries. But there was, no doubt, a garden within the walls, and though it is now much eroded, corn may have been grown on the soil of Christ's Saddle between the two peaks. An eighteenth-century historian of Kerry maintained that Christ's Saddle had been cultivated and that ridges of the plots where corn had been grown were visible then inside the cashel. Vegetables, flour and water and bread were the chief items of the austere diet of Celtic monasticism, but in spite of the Pachomian Rule, flesh seems to have been allowed. In St. Columba's monastery on the Scottish island of Iona, they ate oxen, sheep, seals, and fish. On Skellig they could have had the seals and the fish, and they perhaps ate the puffins which breed on the island, as well as gannets from Little Skellig.

I was doubtful at first whether the steps and the stone paths were as old as the monastery, the buildings of which would go back, as I say, at least to the eighth or seventh century. Long after the monastery had been deserted and up to the eighteenth century, Skellig Michael was an island to which pilgrims came and followed a journey of the Stations of the Cross, which ended on the high peak where the pilgrims, one by one, squeezed out through a cleft called the Needles' Eye and reached to a rock hanging over the Atlantic on which a cross is engraved. The steps cover the island, go up and down and round and across the precipices. Here and there a landfall has carried them away, here and there they vanish under sea-pink. I thought they might belong to the later centuries of pilgrimage, but the monks certainly built stone paths in other monasteries, and I suspect that building them on Skellig and keeping them in order were skilful and dangerous parts of that labour by which they mortified their bodies.

Of these Irish soldiers of Christ, living in a discipline severe beyond that of any army, we know at least one thing unprovided for in the rule St. Pachomius laid down. We know they wrote poems, or that some of them wrote poems; and these poems embody a clean-swept vision of delight in their calling, their religion, and the natural order created by the God they worshipped. One of these poems, a late one, though it was supposed to have been written by St. Columba or Collum Cille, applies so much to Skellig Michael that you should search it out among the fine translations in Kenneth Jackson's *Early Celtic Nature Poetry*. I shall leave that to you, and say a little of the slender history of Skellig Michael.

It is not possible to tell exactly when the monastery was founded or by whom. The bay across from the Skelligs is called St. Finnian's Bay, and the foundation has been given, though not, I think, with much authority, to St. Finian, the great 'tutor of the saints of Ireland', the instructor of St. Brendan the Navigator and of St. Columba. Finnian died in 549. The monastery may indeed have been founded by him or by one of his disciples. Finnian deepened and advanced the monastic life and made it more strict, and his disciples founded a good many island monasteries in which the life of contemplation was still further removed from the distractions and divisions of men. About 822, according to a story repeated in various annals, the Vikings raided Skellig Michael, climbed the steps into the cloud, and took off with them a monk named Edgall, but Skellig was not yet deserted and there are records in the *Annals of the Four Masters* of the death of monks or abbots on Skellig in 950 and 1044. Perhaps the monastery was occupied up to the Anglo-Norman seizure and settlement of Ireland, perhaps till later. It is still venerated. Stories about it are still current. Our boatmen told us, as Skellig was beginning to fade back to blue on the horizon, of the man who had taken water from one of the two wells within the cashel walls and how the water would not boil in his kettle. He told us—which is true enough—that the gannets from Little Skellig never settle on Skellig Michael; and in Charles Smith's *State of the County of Kerry*, published in 1756, you will find a story that 'no bird hath the power to fly over that part of it where the chapels and walls stand, without first alighting on the ground, which they walk gently over, and then take wing'.

I spent most of a day on Skellig Michael and came away reluctantly enough. Militant Protestants have had much to say of the selfishness and defeatism of the monastic life. I don't know. I am neither Protestant, except by upbringing, nor Catholic, but is it not moving to a degree, and not merely to a romantic degree, when we think of that withdrawn life in the wilderness of islands, off these Irish coasts, off Scotland, off Wales, off Brittany, in the Isles of Scilly, in the Farne Islands, and far up in the north in the Westmann Islands, off Iceland? When we think of the quiet of that selfless and hard devotion to an end which is superhuman? Moving about the coasts of Kerry afterwards, I understood what a symbol Skellig Michael must have been to those who were neither monks nor clergy, seeing it on the horizon, a single or a double peak, but always blue, always or often, with its nimbus of white cloud, its trailing coif of holiness.

When we climbed down the steps, the last sound I heard on Skellig Michael was one which had been familiar to the monks, the cheeping (all the other birds had gone) of a late brood of Mother Carey's chickens from a deep hole under the stone.

Third Programme, 1949

6

CULBONE AND 'KUBLA KHAN'

CULBONE IS A PARISH—a very small parish, containing a very small church, a very few farms, a very few cottages, some hill-top, some wood, some cliff, some foreshore; and no village at all. It is in West Somerset, along that strange coast which goes from Minehead to Porlock, then to Culbone, then on to Lynton and Lynmouth.

The lands of Culbone lift themselves quickly out of the sea and up through the woods to sheep-runs a thousand feet higher, which are Exmoor itself. These woods begin just above the water. They are damp, luxuriant, and a little dark and suffocating; and this grey water is the peculiar Severn Sea, the peculiar sea of the Bristol Channel—grey, yes, or mauve, or smoke-colour; often still as death, often noisily grinding its stones, its solid skulls, together along the shore.

Culbone: the name really goes more than anything else for the church, and the valley around, below, and above. More than a valley, it is a deep and gloomy cleft, thrusting back not much more than half a mile from the sea. The woods are thick on either side. From the open fields you drop down just over three hundred feet; and there is the church. Another four hundred feet, and there is the sea. As well as the church there are two cottages, both of them more or less modern; and unless you live in one of the cottages and can drive in a car or a trap along a rough private road through the woods, then you can get to Culbone Church only by walking or riding on horseback through the oak saplings and the ferns, along from Porlock, or down from Ash Farm. Culbone Church, in truth, is a plain, dull, though decent little mediaeval building. I cannot say I care very much whether it is or whether it isn't the smallest complete parish church in England; and I dare say there are times of the day—and night— when one would wish oneself well away from the church in this pit, which is high walled on three sides and open only towards the north, the sea, and Wales.

45

Nearly a sunless pit, in consequence. When I was there, in the evening, I noticed how the sunlight only came about half-way down. The church and the trees above were all in shadow on one side; though, as a man who lived in one of the cottages remarked, that was still a trifle better than living or working in some streets of London which the sun never enters at all. In the church— oak pews, a box pew, a late mediaeval screen, an early font, the twelve commandments on oak panels, a harmonium, a reredos which is by a distinguished architect, C. F. A. Voysey; but, all the same, is not a distinguished piece of Voysey's work. No, it is not the church: it is the situation of the church, the question of why there is a church here, deep down here at Culbone, which is a part of Culbone's peculiarity.

For an answer you must, I think, climb through the woods, and look across the grey sea to Wales, which is only fifteen to twenty miles away. Culbone Church you really should call St. Culbone Church. And St. Culbone? Cornish saints—who they were, more or less, and when they lived—that has been made familiar. One has learnt of Celtic missionary saints who moved from Wales into Cornwall, from Cornwall into Brittany in the sixth century, preaching, converting, founding small monasteries, and oratories; and now and then, and here and there, staying as hermits for a while in retreat. But West Somerset is nearer to Wales than North Cornwall, and these Welsh saints crossed also into Somerset and have left their marks along the coast. Porlock Church has a Welsh saint. So have Congresbury and Timberscombe, and farther east, Corhampton and Watchet.

St. Culbone used to be identified with the great St. Columba; but latterly and more certainly he is equated with the St. Coulban better known across the channel in Brittany. According to their legendary lives, St. Decuman came to Watchet across the Severn Sea on a faggot and Corhampton's St. Carantoc on a stone altar; however St. Coulban made the crossing, one can be certain that the valley below Ash Farm fitted his need exactly as a place of perhaps temporary hermitage. No doubt the valley was wooded then as it is now. Six hundred years or so later, at the time of the Doomsday survey, the manor of Culbone contained twice as much woodland as pasture. Its gloom, solitude, inaccessibility, and beauty, were all precisely proper for meditation on death, life, and eternity.

Culbone has changed in one way. Hundreds of people come there now, and for a hermit it would hardly do. Still, it seems the right place: it seems lonely; it still seems right for this saint whose name is tied to his valley after some fourteen or fifteen hundred years. Culbone also is exactly appropriate for two other men—and one of them a great man indeed—who delighted in the cliffs and the woods, and who must often have splashed, like the saint, through the orange puddles which the rain makes in this Somerset soil. They are Samuel Palmer, the visionary artist, and Samuel Taylor Coleridge, the visionary poet. Palmer, for a few years a superlative interpreter of natural scenery, came to Culbone several times in and after 1835, and left many water-colours of the valley and the church, though they lack the full actuality that presses upon the senses, the full glow, of his best work.

Coleridge: it was near Culbone that Coleridge wrote one of the most celebrated of all English poems—which he first published in 1816 and called 'Kubla Khan; or, A Vision in a Dream'. You will remember how that dream went. It was in 1797. Coleridge, then a young man of twenty-five, and living at Nether Stowey with his wife and child, retired in ill-health, as he said in the original note printed with the poem, 'to a lonely farm-house between Porlock and Lynton'. He had diarrhoea; opium was prescribed, and as he read *Purchas His Pilgrimage* he dozed off at the sentence which begins 'In Xamdu did Cublai Can build a stately Palace'. Asleep, he had the 'most vivid confidence' of composing two to three hundred lines of verse. He woke up, he at once began to write the poem down, when that celebrated 'person on business from Porlock' called at the farm, detained him more than an hour, and left him 'to his no small surprise and mortification' remembering only a few fragments of the rest of the poem. Fifty-three lines. These, at any rate, were on paper, and preserved out of the poem which might have been the most wonderful of its kind in European literature.

Where was the farmhouse? There was nothing to connect it with Culbone until in 1934 a manuscript of 'Kubla Khan', in Coleridge's hand, turned up with extra information about where it was written and how:

'This fragment with a good deal more, not recoverable, composed in a sort of Reverie brought on by two grains of

Opium, taken to check a dysentery, at a Farm House between Porlock and Linton, a quarter of a mile from Culbone Church, in the fall of the year, 1797.'

A quarter of a mile from Culbone Church. When I clambered from the church, and came out on the top, above the woods, above the sea, and in sight of Glamorgan and Pembrokeshire, I didn't myself have much doubt that 'Kubla Khan' was dreamt and written down in the first farmhouse you reach, high in this short valley—Ash Farm, that is to say. It depends upon Coleridge's accuracy. Ash Farm *is* a quarter of a mile up from Culbone Church. Not far off, there is also Parsonage Farm, a quarter of a mile from the church, but that was not a farmhouse in Coleridge's day—so Lord Knebworth tells me, and he lives there. In fact, it had been the rectory till 1791. If Coleridge was not too accurate, it might have been Yearnor Farm to the east or Silcombe to the west; but each one is a good half mile from the church. The westward fork of the valley up from the church is called Withycombe, and here there used to be a house attached to a very small holding—perhaps too poor a house for Coleridge to have stayed at. No. All of the probabilities say it was Ash, an old house in Coleridge's day, where 'Kubla Khan' was written, and where so much more of the poem was dissipated by that untimely arrival from Porlock.

If you are unattracted by most guide-books (I hope you are), if you are cynical about 'associations' (as Coleridge was), and if you think a place should be liked only for itself, and if you have no wish to see Coleridge's old bedroom slippers, do not condemn me too much at this point. Coleridge is not R. D. Blackmore. 'Kubla Khan' is not a fifth-rate poem as *Lorna Doone*, after all, is a fifth-rate novel; and Ash Farm is not the Doone Valley. Scholars have written about the bookish origin of 'Kubla Khan'. They have not considered that Coleridge also read and enjoyed landscape as if it were a book. Landscape suggested to him the states of the human spirit. Landscape was a source of his poems. One projected poem was partly suggested to him by the Valley of Rocks at Lynton, another, a philosophic poem he intended to call 'The Brook', was suggested to him by the streams running down from the Quantocks. So, as he said, he walked on Quantock 'making studies, as the artists call them, and often moulding my thoughts into verse with the objects and imagery immediately before my senses'. Not a little in 'Kubla Khan' was suggested to him, I believe, by what he had seen that day from Ash Farm. He fell asleep on a sentence from the folio book on his knees. But he must also have fallen asleep on that great view towards Wales.

Looking across from the fields above the farmhouse, watching as a light came on in some house in Wales, I could not doubt that the quiet, darkish, smoke-coloured sea, which between Wales and Culbone was a wide lake, helped within Coleridge's vision to suggest that 'sunless sea' into which Alph the sacred river ran, that 'lifeless ocean' into which it entered after its five miles' meandering; I could not doubt that the woods down below, blackening into the cleft which contained the invisible church, helped to suggest the 'forests ancient as the hills', or that the cleft had to do with the poem's 'deep, romantic chasm'.

To say this in no way contradicts the findings about 'Kubla Khan' which J. L. Lowes made in *The Road to Xanadu*. He discovered Coleridge's source of the lifeless and sunless sea in a nether ocean under the roots of the world from which, according to the *Quaestiones Naturales* of Seneca, rivers such as the Alphaeus —the 'Alph' of the poem—and the Nile emerge. Is it wild to fancy Coleridge looking across the Bristol Sea from Ash Farm on a sunless still autumn day and saying to himself 'Seneca's vast sea with winding shores in the depths of earth must be like that?' Another hazard may be a wild one, but I shall risk it—that there *is* a likeness of sound between the words *Culbone*, which we know Coleridge admired above most places, and *Kubla Khan*. I have often found, myself, that in states between waking and dreaming words of similar sound suggest each other and tend to mix or transform the associations which belong to each of them. Perhaps a door must be shut on this, before I hear the well-bred derision of scholarship, and begin blushing.

That Culbone was the only place which had to do with Coleridge's vision, over and above the books he had been reading, I would not maintain; but I do say that it was one of them (elsewhere I have explained my belief that other elements in the poem were partly given to Coleridge by the huge valley,

D   49

the gardens and the mansion of Hafod in Wales); and I do say
you should visit Ash Farm, read the poem again, as well as
The Road to Xanadu, and judge for yourself. Perhaps, though,
the best reason for walking to Culbone is that the conjunction
of sea and coomb and wood and steepness makes one of the
most extraordinarily suggestive landscapes anywhere in England,
suggesting the quick and the dead, life and lifelessness. St.
Coulban, Samuel Palmer, and Coleridge, a hermit, a painter, and
a poet, who knew nothing of each other in relation to Culbone—
they are three of the witnesses to that fact.

West of England, 1948

7

PADDINGTON STATION

CAN YOU REMEMBER when you first saw Paddington Station? I realize I must have seen it first in 1911; when my father, I am inclined to think in a clerical frock-coat and a top hat, took me from Looe to London, and from London to a school in Kent. I know I must have seen Paddington. But I do not remember it at all. In fact, all I know of that journey is going in a cab—a horse cab—across London to Victoria, and seeing from the cab, not the things my father was pointing out to me— the Marble Arch no doubt and Park Lane—but two not very large plastery lions walking towards each other along a wall, which flanked a house opposite Hyde Park. The lions are still walking along, with their tails stuck out behind them. Every time I came to London during the war, when houses were disappearing between visit and visit, I looked, as I passed along that now familiar route out of Paddington, in a taxi, for my two lions. It was comforting each time to find them neither broken nor destroyed; though the bombs exploded pretty close.

Indeed, thinking about Paddington, do we, I ask, ever see it, whether we are six, as I was in 1911, or sixty-six? From the time that I was six until I was eighteen I reached Paddington many times a year, going from Cornwall to school and coming home— that was better—coming home to Cornwall. Now I go through Paddington—quite blindly—about once a week. We go through Paddington. From the arrival platforms we hurriedly go through its drab, its greasy back-areas, by taxi out into Praed Street, or we walk quickly to the hole which leads Underground. Going from Paddington, we see a little more, between the ticket window or one of the bookstalls on No. 1, or the tea-room on No. 1, and the train. Indeed, No. 1 Platform *is* Paddington—particularly for West Country people; and Paddington does count, exterritorially, as a part of the West of England. No. 1 Platform, above all, is Cornish, is Devonshire, is Somerset property—up to a point. Paddington, don't you feel, is an emotional word, connected for us with those pleasures of *coming back*. But words and emotions are not things that we look at. I knew visually one item and another, from the whale-back (which one sees—often with relief —from a taxi cutting up towards Praed Street) to that bronze statue of a soldier on No. 1, which is one of the dullest of all dull lumps of public bronze. (I once talked about that statue to Eric Gill, who said gravely that it marked, didn't I realize it, a great advance in the spiritual development of the sculptor who designed it. Until then all his figures had had their legs together. The soldier on No. 1 was the first to have his legs apart.) And of course you and I know that Paddington is built in several aisles with glass in the roof, that Paddington is really all roof supported on pillars, all painted—but have you looked enough to be quite sure what the colour is?

All painted drab—a pale brown—drab and chocolate. But the details? The general and the detailed effects? Paddington is not one of the oldest, or older stations on the old G.W.R. The platforms did not come into use till 1854, and the station was not complete, even then, until 1855. It is a Victorian station, as the railways were Victorian, and were immense and magnetic in the mind of the Victorians. Look up at Paddington. How else did Brunel, the engineer of the railway, the engineer of the station, think of it than as a Cathedral of Locomotion with aisles and transepts? Paddington—in 1855: it was modernity, progress, certainty; it was England *über alles*. It was still modern in 1861, when a picture dealer had commissioned W. P. Frith to paint his celebrated realistic representation of Paddington. Frith was to get for the picture and the copyright 8000 guineas; on top of that another 750 guineas, since at the dealer's request he had forgone his right to exhibit 'Paddington' at the Royal Academy. The sum, £9187, 10s., was the greatest ever paid to an artist for a modern picture. *That* was what this railway cathedral meant nearly a hundred years ago—as a dealer you could get your money back on a painting of a railway terminus even if it cost you more than nine thousand pounds. So you can be sure that Brunel meant us to look and not just to pass through. He meant us to look at the incised ornament on the walls. He meant us to look at the slender pillars and the pseudo-Gothic ornaments bolted to them, to look at the pattern of stars and holes in the cast-iron spans which curve overhead. He meant us to look—look, look up at the stars, look at all the glass roofing hanging in the air, which I, Isambard Kingdom Brunel, have adopted from the new and wonderful Crystal Palace, under which our Great Exhibition was exhibited five years ago.

And what do we do—we go through your Cathedral-Palace of Locomotion, Mr. Brunel, and see nothing. We clank past Kensal Green (it's true that we cannot see the cemetery any more from the train)—and we do not think of you lying there by your railway.

'Life at a Railway Station'—so Firth's picture was to be called; and I have to say that in my time, in my frequentation of the platforms, it has been rather the people, rather the life I have noticed, rather incidents to do with others and myself.

Smaller stations farther west—in a way one allows them a personality which Paddington is too big to have acquired. Bristol, a wide, platitudinous station, with a dignified shirt-front, a middle-aged, solid business-man, with a smell about him of the fish-glue of his own factory. Liskeard—cold and casual; but I liked Liskeard for three things, for the way the trains came curving out of Cornwall and charging up hill, for the flow of cotoneaster over the rock, and for a rarer plant which used to grow above the up-platform. Penzance, into which the first train steamed as late as 1866—open, friendly, clean, a full stop, a compulsory all-change, with a small notice saying when the next boat leaves Penzance harbour for the Isles of Scilly. A station from which you can go on, in a real sense, only by sea or by that bus which leads to the airport.

Swindon—an early station, and believe me, once a genteel, respectable station of local stone, turned only by neglect and by tasteless additions into a slut. Do you know the Swindon refreshment rooms?—or dejection rooms? Can you picture them—it takes some doing through the cigarette ends—elegant and smart with arabesque walls and ceiling, and columns 'painted after a recent invention to resemble inlaid wood'? Full of elegant and smart people who were forced to eat at Swindon, since all trains by agreement with the caterers had to stop there for ten minutes, at least—until 1875?

Was the coffee better than it is now? Brunel, a year after the station opened, wrote to the caterer:

'Dear Sir,

I assure you Mr. Player was wrong in supposing that I thought you purchased inferior coffee. I thought I said to him that I was surprised you should buy such bad roasted corn. I did not believe you had such a thing as coffee in the place; I am certain that I never tasted any. I have long ceased to make complaints at Swindon. I avoid taking anything there when I can help it.

Yours faithfully,

I. K. Brunel.'

Bad roasted corn: modern railway coffee is made of old roasted linoleum. Still, this worn slut of a Swindon station was once part of the glory, and for us the glory has gone. The railways for us are not at all what they were for the Victorians, the symbol of a new world of power and danger. Maddening, wrote Charles Kingsley, was the exquisite motion of a yacht springing away close-hauled on a freshening breeze, 'but not so maddening as the new motion of our age—the rush of the express-train, when the live iron pants and leaps and roars through the long chalk cutting; and white mounds gleam cold a moment against the sky and vanish; and rocks, and grass, and bushes, fleet by in dim-blended lines; and the long hedges revolve like the spokes of a gigantic wheel; and far below, meadows, and streams, and home-steads, with all their lazy old-world life, open for an instant, and then flee away; while awestruck, silent, choked with the mingled sense of pride and helplessness, we are swept on by that great pulse of England's life-blood, rushing down her iron veins; and dimly out of the future looms the fulfilment of our primaeval mission, to conquer and subdue the earth, and space too, and time, and all things. . . . Yes, great railroads, and great railroad age, who would exchange you, with all your sins, for any other time?'

The wonder has gone; and the grand expression of the wonder. A hundred years have made the railways dirty, ugly, and ordinary; the railways have been so greedy for advertising revenue that the deliberate dignity of Brunel's railway architecture has been smeared over with posters. And the triumphal archway into Euston has been concealed.

Of course we do not notice Paddington any more. We are too used to it, and too used to all the other terminals; and if we were not, too much has been done to make us wish not to see them. That is why I think of Paddington as an emotion, and not as a place or a building; why I think of it rather in terms of people— the Emperor of Abyssinia up from Bath, wandering sadly, in a soft hat, towards the Great Western Hotel; generals and field-marshals of the German army and air force walking stiffly on No. 2 Platform, and getting into the train which took them back from Nuremberg to their prison camp in Wales (may I say, having seen it from the corridor, that one field-marshal was reading the *Spectator* and another the *New Statesman*). And on Paddington No. 1, in the Riviera, in a corner seat, something that happened to me before the first of the world wars—meeting, as I came back from my prep. school in Kent, my brothers from their public school in Surrey, with a friend of theirs who lived also in Cornwall; myself, aged eight, settling down in that corner to a seven-penny edition of *King Solomon's Mines*, and this large, impressive stranger, old and mature to me, saying to my brothers, 'Isn't he young to be reading that?'

For me, on Paddington, it was one of the greatest and sweetest moments of a lifetime.

West of England, 1948

8

DURHAM CATHEDRAL

NOT LONG AFTER 1540, on behalf of the King, three commissioners of a new world, the new secular world of the
Reformation ousting the Middle Ages, climbed up the
hill to the cathedral and convent of Durham. They were Dr.
Ley, Dr. Henley, and Master Blythman, and they broke up the
shrine of St. Cuthbert which stood at the eastern end of the
cathedral between a delicate mediaeval screen and the long transept known as the Chapel of the Nine Altars. The ornaments
and the jewels about the saint were ripped off by their attendant
lapidaries, the painting of Christ seated upon a rainbow was no
doubt destroyed, and the silver bells were pulled down. Then
coming nearer to St. Cuthbert's sacred body 'and finding', so the
account runs, 'the chiste that he did lie in very strongly bound
with irone', one of the lapidaries 'did taike a great forehammer
of a smyth, and did breake the said chiste open'.

I read this on the train up from the south. The train was now
on the railway viaduct, and I saw the cathedral for the first time.
I looked across to the black ziggurat, the great rocky platform of
holiness which supported the cathedral. I realized how with
that blow of the hammer St. Cuthbert had ceased to be a vessel
filled with deity; how at last after a long interval in which the
character of the religion celebrated within his church had twice
been changed, those three commissioners and that goldsmith
with the sledge-hammer unwittingly had founded, so to say, an
abstract, a secular interest in the analysis of the style of Durham
Cathedral. The clump of the hammer prepared Durham for an
enfeebled entry into text-books of architecture.

In these text-books, architecture becomes an abstraction from
buildings, the history of styles an abstraction from the actuality
of purpose. Durham, the books say, is a wonderful building.
Durham is one of the most important buildings in Northern
Europe. In Durham we have the first surviving example of the
rib-vaulted nave, the nave arched across with a stone roof. Yet

I realized, looking over the chimneys of the city, that Durham must indeed be itself. It must indeed be this particular cathedral in itself, in its stones. It must be the cathedral surrounded by this black river and these black woods, rising out of this particular city, it must be the cathedral built to cover the so long un-corrupted body of that saint, and that vessel of deity, Cuthbert of Lindisfarne. It was not likely to be only another, if most notable, Romanesque building. Raised with whatever engineering skill, tending to whatever stylistic changes, with whatever later trim-mings, I expected to find Durham Cathedral still, to the sensitive, the outer covering or the external shrine of that body of the saint. St. Cuthbert's magic body had summoned all the yellow blocks of sandstone.

So I knew that it was with St. Cuthbert, with the part occasioning the whole, that I had to begin. Soberly (because I cannot count myself a religious man), and even stylistically and architecturally, my pilgrimage from the platform of Durham railway station had to be towards his body; which by the King's pleasure had been replaced in the cathedral in a plain coffin. Very well. I walked down through the February drizzle into the trough of the world, over the stone streets, into the dirty mess of cheap jewellery, discarded football papers, and army surplus stores, and chimneys of brown smoke. I walked across the bridge, and up and out of the trough under the castle of the Prince Bishops of Durham, taking to the narrow mediaeval dirt of Moatside Lane. I was up on the ziggurat, up on the platform of holiness and surprisingly alone with the sky and the outer walls of St. Cuthbert. 'In Egypt' (to change from the ziggurat to the pyra-mid) 'the creator was said to have emerged from the waters of chaos and to have made a mound of clay upon which he could stand', a mound stylized into the pyramid. Here was a creator's mound of rock, or a creator's primaeval hill, washed around with the river; and I walked over the hill and stepped through the north door.

No further knowledge of Durham is ever going to excel the shock of this first entry, of these first steps *down* into the cathedral. I am never going to feel more of the strength and weight and alien barbarism and the physical coldness of Durham. At once the immense rhythms of the arcade, the immense solidity and the stone vaulting and the stone floor are felt to be the means of enclosing deity; or rather the means of providing an eternal solidness inside of which deity could be enticed to dwell. Deity, in fact, had been laid there concentrated in St. Cuthbert's body. A bizarre deity. He is present like a dragon in its cave. He is a deity of action and of power, of the axe and the thunder, male rather than female, or androgynal, Old Testament more than New, pagan as well as Christian. He is incalculable and he is to be feared underneath these pillars. So how appropriate that marble line across the floor, beyond which women were not allowed into the nave! How appropriate the contradiction between Jehovah's nave, where I was now standing, and the elegant and lively Galilee of the Virgin Mary behind my back, the Lady Chapel poised over the river at the west end of the cathedral! If you walk along the edge of a plantation, the slender tree-trunks nearest to you appear to move, to move past the slender trunks beyond them. It is like that as you walk among the slender arcades of the Galilee. The pillars move, the architecture seems alive and gay. But in the nave once more the pillars are fixed and immobile in a great solemnity.

Yet the Galilee, built rather later than the nave, is perhaps contrast rather than contradiction. We have to keep contradiction for the moment when we turn out from either of the entrances into the Galilee and look down the long Romanesque aisles to the thirteenth-century Chapel of the Nine Altars. The nave and the choir (so far as it is still the Romanesque choir) belong to that bizarre deity who is a god of the earth, hardly to be recognized, so it seemed to me, as the Christian God. The nave was the entry to the cave within the cave. But the Chapel of the Nine Altars, which is an eastern transept beyond the choir, is not really Durham at all. Added a hundred years later, up it leaps in the slender lines of marble and sandstone as if here at least the more familiar God were both in and above His delightful creation. This new and authentically Christian deity will no doubt elude the stretched fingers, and become for so many people so infinite that he will dissipate and disappear altogether into the sky. But if we go back from the Nine Altars, and past the choir, and return into the coldness and grandeur of the nave, we are closer again to Avebury and Stonehenge. We are back in a north European paganism injected with Christianity from the south; or we may call it an aberrant, or at least a rudimentary Christianity. We walk among the pillars—walk under the pillars —more like woodlice who feel the dampness, chilliness, and hardness of stone, and not at all like the universal Christians of the true Middle Ages, the Christians of that Chapel of the Nine Altars who are bold enough to think of love and aspiration and a personal union with the divine. The pillars of this cave, around and above me, fluted, zig-zagged, spiralled, diamonded, and plain, are so many immense trunks of rock. They grow downward into their roots rather than up into their branches and foliage, of which upward growth the novel rib-vaulting over my head is no more than an intimation. The lines gouged ornamentally out of these trunks of sandstone, and filled with shadow, only emphasize that they are trunks of a grimness, indeed of a solemn dismay.

Gothic Christianity may be implicit in these rocks shaped into stones; but St. Cuthbert himself and the Prince Bishops, William of St. Carileph (who held the see from 1081 to 1096) and Ralph Flambard (who held it from 1097 to 1128), under whom so much of Durham was deposited, all three of them knew that deity of the rocks, that deity who may seem to us to have been grotesque and jealous and local, and too lacking in tenderness. They would have been astounded, one may think, and abashed at the rich shrine which rose over the coffin beneath the delicacies of the Neville screen. They would not have cared for the green marble 'limned and quilted with gold', or for the jewellery or for those six silver bells which rang when the cover of the shrine was raised, and 'did make such a good sound that itt did stir all the people's harts that was within the church to repair unto itt'. Upon the platform where the shrine stood beneath the screen and within the Chapel of the Nine Altars, we have to think of the Virgin holding the child and of the pink and the green and the youthfulness of the mediaeval lyric, the lyric of the south. In the centre of the nave, and in the aisles, feeling the weight and contemplating the writhing lines within the sandstone of darker rust and orange, I remember those squat figures of the Sheila-na-gig, whose smiles in the wrong place so curiously ornament many Romanesque churches; and afterwards, in the train going back to the south, I thought of that northern poem, the 'Lyke Wake

Dirge', chanted over dead bodies, in which the soul knows nothing of love, but proceeds by the gorse points of Whinny Muir to the Brig o' Dread (over hell's flame), and on to the fires of Purgatory:

> If ever thou gavest meat or drink,
>   Every nighte and alle,
> The fire shall never make thee shrink;
>   And Christe receive thy saule.

> If meat or drink thou ne'er gavest nane,
>   Every nighte and alle,
> The fire will burn thee to the bare bane,
>   And Christe receive thy saule.

And I thought of how that poem has been set so fiercely and appropriately by Benjamin Britten.

Once, it seems to me, all that is possessed in the mind, we can attend to Durham Cathedral in its mass and in all of its parts, in its barbarous grandeur and its by no means surprising endurance, when by religious rights and changes it should have been pulled down long ago. Of course, elements of that peculiarity of religion which planted the stone tree-trunks of Durham into the ground did subsist beneath the mediaeval religion which raised the Chapel of the Nine Altars. They subsisted beneath the more frail and frozen religion within which James Wyatt evolved his restorations of Durham at the close of the eighteenth century; and they may even be supposed to subsist beneath that religion of the nineteen-forties which has not felt the much viler and more acid incongruity of the miscoloured windows so lately inserted at the west end of both of the Romanesque aisles.

But Durham has been emphatic enough in its nature to ensure that these elements are felt with a particular local strength up here on the ziggurat. The original force, for example, has kept most of the dead outside the walls, leaving the cathedral almost entirely for St. Cuthbert. And though his shrine was broken up, and though the sledge-hammer did come down upon his coffin, St. Cuthbert is still there in his cathedral. He was replaced, after all, by the King's pleasure.

Third Programme, 1949

9

A WINDOW IN THE AIR

THE CAR has been an instrument—even a symbol—of
laissez-faire democracy; one man, one car. The aeroplane
suggests to me the dictatorship of the masses, in which the
power goes to a few top dogs who fly about on their official mass-
democratic business in these expensive and peculiar instruments.
The ruck of us are enticed into planes when there are wars to be
fought and bombs to be released. So in spite of the perpetual
noise of aeroplanes in the air, the eastern, the northern, the
southern, and the western air, most of us stick to our native
ground. I cannot claim yet to being a patriarch or even as old
as Mr. Shaw, but I belong to the age before aeroplanes. When I
was a child I went to parties by waggonette, a pleasant means of
travel which enabled you to search for the Pole Star or to try
counting all of the Seven Sisters. I think there was not a car at
all in my parish in Cornwall until 1918. We believed that one
plane had passed over the parish in the first war, and before that
I remember waiting with a crowd, a huge crowd, on Plymouth
Hoe intent upon witnessing the arrival of somebody's plane from
France. Occasionally since then I have needed to abandon the
ground—flying from London to Paris, the Tiber to Sardinia,
Copenhagen to Croydon; but I am an ordinary civilian who does
not hop the Atlantic to the United Nations or fly on trade missions
to Moscow Airport. So, until last September, I had never made
a casual trip, by air, across a familiar terrain. I had never done
such a still revolutionary thing (revolutionary for most of us) as
ring up and hire a plane as one rings up a taxi. Then an impulse
came and I did so. Two miles away from our front door, in
North Wiltshire, a plane waited for us on the aerodrome at Clyffe
Pypard, below the Marlborough Downs. We climbed into it—a
minute single-engined monoplane—circled out of the east wind,
and set off in the direction of America.

There was my window. But I do not recollect that I did much
looking out of it at first. Like all of the occasionally airborne, I

had to overcome that sense of insecurity and apprehension. I had one insecure and apprehensive child on my lap, another insecure and apprehensive child in the seat alongside. One could not do justice to the first prospects of the West which curved underneath, though I noticed the sweep and shadow and folding of the Downs, where they dropped below that obelisk to Sir William Petty, between Avebury and Calne. It was by the time the pilot turned and shouted 'Bath', and pointed, that we were getting the sense of the thing straight, were beginning to use the window, and push into the background that this mild adventure might mean the end of our family and ourselves. I had wondered if the West Regional news-reader might not include thirty seconds of the crash in the evening bulletin. Moreover, in those first twenty minutes of Wiltshire, more than the immense noise and the apprehension had been uncomfortable. The sun was full onto us, and we were all, especially the child on my lap, bothered with stuffiness and damp. Beyond Bath, clouds began to belly between ourselves and the sun; and the children were dozing off.

I began to notice the world. Familiarities began to show themselves in a surprising, comprehensive, unfamiliar way. Just ahead of us a long narrow slit divided dark land (we were not very high above that land) and cloud nearly as dark. Greenness and sunshine were gleaming to us through the slit, at a much lower level; and I realized, with a start, it was Sedgemoor we were coming to, the Mendips we were crossing and leaving. The thought came to me of Thomas Hardy's own favourite among his poems, 'A Trampwoman's Tragedy', with its celebration of 'sad Sedgemoor', and 'Blackmoor wide, And where the Parret ran'.

'We'd faced the gusts on Mendip ridge'—so had we in our plane, the Mendip ridge was the lower boundary of the dark slit—'Had crossed the Yeo unhelped by bridge'. And we indeed were crossing the Yeo with no such aid, were now heading, though I did not tumble to it, towards Taunton. It is an apprehensive poem, that tragedy of Thomas Hardy's. The clouds, the darkness of the land, and lurking feelings about being so far above the land fitted well with the poem just then.

About now, I began to see I was in danger of missing the

memory of sights and scenes—that Mendip ridge, that clouded bulk of the Quantocks which we had faced and turned our backs upon. I had a pen, but no paper; so I pulled out one of those brown bags marked 'For Air Sickness', and began to make notes and sketches on it for the remaining seventy minutes or so in the air. I never had asked the pilot which route he would be taking; and, by the way, I have not yet revealed our objective. Somewhat deterred by the sea-passage from Penzance in the s.s. *Scillonian*, we were going to the Isles of Scilly; and I was not sure whether we were to cut across between Exmoor and Dartmoor, and come down the north coast of Cornwall; or whether we should turn south. Recognizing by its curve down below the municipal building at Taunton—that didn't give the answer; but it was hinted very soon, when the ground began to come up and when we were sliding, I realized, over the Blackdowns, low enough past the Wellington Monument to see the bare yellow top between the heather.

Then, the Exe Estuary. Clearly we were going much as the Great Western Railway goes; and there indeed was the Great Western, there was a train, a Devon and Cornwall express creeping along in and out of the tunnels; and the wing tip of the plane was gradually eating it up. We were not so very fast, as planes fly, but we were faster than the train, which was a satisfactory feeling.

The children were coming to life. One had been sick, before he had gone to sleep. But now we were out at sea, turning the corner by Dawlish, and the bumps and jerks had come to an end. The progress was level and smooth. The children were sick no more, and sleepy no more, and began using the window. It was just about here, between Dawlish and Teignmouth, that I saw the most exquisite of all the sights between Wiltshire and Scilly. I drew it hastily, with a note, on the bag marked 'Air Sickness'. It was the line of anchovy-red cliffs, topped with green, and over them a long, long roll of full white clouds curving up from the land over the sea. The sea—the sea was blue, almost to being black.

From Tor Bay, we left the sea, and cut across land to Plymouth, and the whitened line of the breakwater. Mostly now we had cloud between ourselves and the land, and cloud above, though the lower cloud parted both for the Dart, wriggling between its woods, and for Plymouth Sound. Cornwall we did not, to my disappointment, see so much of, though we went low over the green of Looe Island, and shot past the front door of Polperro, looking through the window past Chapel Rock and up into the harbour and the coomb. Somewhere past Fowey, the pilot decided that the children should see the upper heaven, so, watching the needle, we climbed steadily through grey cloud, broke into the sun, and cruised along, far above an invisible Cornish coast, and over a level sea of white cloud; having at last that wonderful sense of freedom and security which comes in the air when the navel string to that earth one belongs to is cut and the earth cannot be seen any more.

Green fields beyond Helston were the next visible land; and soon, St. Michael's Mount, in the evening sunlight; Penzance, over on the right, and the final cliffs towards Land's End. Then a speck down in the sea. No, not the Isles of Scilly; but the s.s. *Scillonian*. As the pilot had thought we should climb into the upper heaven, so he thought now we should have a look at the sea and the *Scillonian*. Down, down steeply to within fifty feet of the masts, and the *Scillonian* pitching and heaving, and only three or four hardier passengers on deck to wave.

Cornwall and England abandoned. An immense Atlantic, an immense western sky; this was the serenest part of all the journey, climbing steadily up over the Atlantic into a now clear sky, and flying on peacefully and steadily towards a wall of sunset, golden lines over green and pink, over grey. Down in that sunset were the islands, still not to be detected. My brown-paper bag and my mind were overcrowded with glimpses, overcrowded with those familiarities turned into the unfamiliar—churches, towns, villages, the white bang of the high tide against Looe Island, black hills, grey cliffs and red cliffs, interchanges over the West of darkness and of light. Yet—through our small square window, it had been an extraordinary grasping of all of the West, at least of the whole length of the West, within two hours or so. A long length of our own country thoroughly modified by all the generations who have lived in it, made fields and roads and villages, and towns, and large sprawling funguses like Torquay. All the generations have humanized this length, but not pushed the humanizing so far yet as to have soiled and spoiled it, except in a corner here and there. And these corners are lost in what is really an immensity of variation, as various as the people of North Wiltshire and Land's End—so immense that it must always remain much as it is. Yet now it was less the sensations of the past than the sensation of the moment, in this Atlantic serenity. A feel of comfortable, timeless isolation—even more of comfortable eternity, enjoyed now, neither in prospect nor retrospect, enforced by the steady rounding noise of our progress.

After two hours and twenty minutes, the plane sloped towards the sunset. In all the sights I had nearly lost the sense of being carried by the plane. The islands and the wrinkled sea came up. The desert Eastern Islands, St. Martin's and the red-and-white Day Mark, the dark green of the conifers of Tresco, the double peak of Samson. The plane circled St. Mary's twice; and there we were, out in the Atlantic, out—and safe—on the minute airfield, and in a few minutes were scurrying in a launch across the darkening lagoon, across the full tide, to one of the Off Islands.

West of England, 1947

10

EDWARD GODDARD

GARDENER AND ANTIQUARY

EW PEOPLE outside Wiltshire may have heard of Edward
Hungerford Goddard, who was born in 1854 and died not
so long ago at a great age, over ninety. His life was not a
spectacle or dramatic, but it is worth celebration. I have long
thought of him, so to say, as an ideal perennial, a man of interests
rooted into his soil, a remarkable gardener, perhaps because those
interests went altogether beyond gardening and were almost without limit. I knew him myself only a little, much as I knew *of* him,
which is another matter. But it was with a sadness that I heard
over the fields between his house and mine the bell of his own
church. The bell tolling for him turned one to Thomas Hardy's
poem on the death of the Dorset poet and clergyman William
Barnes. Hardy stood on the path as Barnes was carried out to
his churchyard, and as the sun flashed on the brass fittings of his
coffin:

> Looking hard and harder I knew what it meant—
> The sudden shine sent from the livid east scene;
> It meant the west mirrored by the coffin of my friend there,
> Turning to the road from his green,
>
> To take his last journey forth—he who in his prime
> Trudged so many a time from that gate athwart the land!
> Thus a farewell to me he signalled on his grave-way,
> As with a wave of his hand.

I do not know that Edward Goddard ever wrote a poem, except
comic poems to amuse his children; but in much else how like
he was to Barnes in the neighbouring county, how well the two
of them would have agreed! Both were parish priests, both
gardeners, both antiquaries, around both revolved the archaeological affairs of a county, both drew sustenance, like yews in a
churchyard, from the past and from the earth of their own
counties—Goddard even more so than Barnes.

For more than half a century Goddard was vicar—till he retired to Devizes in 1935—of Clyffe Pypard, a tree-enclosed village under the guardianship of that chalk escarpment which runs across North Wiltshire. In this village, cottages, inn (the Goddard Arms), manor house, vicarage, and church are all close together. The manor itself a Goddard had purchased of a London alderman in 1530, after making money in the wool trade on the Downs above, towards Berkshire. So Edward Goddard was vicar at Clyffe, where the manor had descended from father to son for nine generations. His grandfather and his great-grand-father—both had been vicars and Lords of the Manor. There is a story recorded of that great-grandfather. He had presented to the living a friend he had made as an undergraduate at Oxford. They quarrelled—not an unfamiliar situation in a parish. When the vicar died at last in 1769, the squire affirmed he 'would have no more vicars at Clyffe', and though well beyond the flush of his youth he was ordained, and became vicar himself.

So much for the emotional sense into which Goddard was born, and in which he lived his long and even life. When he stood in Clyffe Church, there he was in his surplice above forty-three Goddards in the vault. When he christened a child at the font, it was at a font carved by his own father. When he crossed the churchyard (which he made into a garden nearly as charming as his own) to the wall-gate opening into the vicarage grounds, he passed by a beech, still alive, planted 180 years ago by the ancestor who 'would have no more vicars at Clyffe'. Goddard himself was born not at Clyffe but at Alderton, on the border of Wiltshire and Gloucestershire; but he grew up near Clyffe, in the next vicarage of Hilmarton. There his father, a younger son of the Goddards, was also something of an antiquary and a man inquisitive into many things. In 1886 Goddard married his cousin, who was daughter of the vicar of Clyffe; three years before, his uncle at the manor house—the vicar having died—had presented him to the living. The vicarage was his wife's home for nearly all of her life. There he stayed himself until he was over eighty, and into the churchyard alongside he was brought back from Devizes to be buried.

He was a small man, at least in old age, with a quick face which reminded me of a lizard or of a wise and wrinkled hawk.

I saw him on several occasions, in his garden, his pulpit, and else-where; but two occasions stick. His cousin died at the manor house. There was a sale. Family accumulations—even to family pictures—were jumbled in a marquee in front of the house. Sitting among the crowd and the dealers, in a clerical frock-coat, with his glasses on the end of his nose and a string curving from the glasses, outwardly unemotional, Goddard was bidding for things, I supposed at the time, he had no wish to see dispersed among strangers. Early in the war, I went to have tea with him in his retirement at Devizes. He was more than eighty then, but full of intellect and energy. He showed me a photograph of Clyffe vicarage as it was when he became vicar, a raw Victorian house surrounded by pale wintry fields, not by the triumph of a garden he had created through half a century. Then—'Would I like to see the new garden?' This little old man put on a sleeve-less leather coat, took a shooting-stick, and hustled me into this new garden around his brick villa, and introduced me to plant after plant. I asked the name of an unfamiliar species with blue flowers which he had brought over from the old garden at Clyffe. Making a gesture of annoyance with one hand, he had to admit he could not remember. 'And you won't remember names yourself when you are my age.'

His garden had been an historic continuation, since the impulse to make it had come to him from one of the most celebrated clerical gardeners in the West, Canon Ellacombe, of Bitton, near Bristol, who gave him plants and cuttings. When he left Clyffe in 1935 he was growing some 1300 species, and there still flourished in the garden, for example, the *Lilium umbellatum* he had collected during his honeymoon in 1886 on the mountains above Menaggio in Italy and primulas from Monte Generoso. The garden was a curious blend of gardening before and after Gertrude Jekyll, a mixture of Impressionist colour (I dare say Goddard would have thought the art of the Impressionists, even of Monet, an outrageous revolution) and of Victorian evergreen. 'Too many conifers' I thought to myself when I went round it, yet it was a 'natural' garden of cunning concealments and openings, paths and surprises, warmth and shadow, merging into wildernesses; and now it has gone the way of vicarage gardens into weeds and ruin.

As a parish priest Goddard created a local legend of solidity and omniscience; and he was deeply respected, as educated parsons of his kind were—and are where they still exist. Wiltshire archaeology, as I say, revolved around him, midway between antiquarianism and the scientific archaeology of the times of O. G. S. Crawford and Gordon Childe. He carried on a county tradition of infinite curiosity about the local past and much else which began in Wiltshire with John Aubrey. For years, fifty-two years, he edited the magazine of the Wiltshire Archaeological Society, for years he cherished the museum and the library at Devizes and helped to make them one of the important local collections of England. He was not so much a writer as a tireless excavator of facts, a tireless accumulator of knowledge. Nothing was foreign to his benign curiosity, plant, bird, insect, Bronze Age loom-weight, or a mediaeval charter. His name crops up with some fact attached to it in book after book of local studies. Once in a boarding-house in a Welsh spa I picked up a book published long ago on British serpents, in which the boarders had scribbled their rummy scores. On one page was printed a note about snakes in Wiltshire: 'Though I have lived all my life in North Wilts I have never seen an adder. The ring snake, on the other hand, is common—Rev. Ed. H. Goddard, Clyffe Vicarage, Wootton Bassett.' His eyes, his hands were always busy. On a picnic with his children an ant would run off with a crumb, and would have to be tracked to the end of its journey, an insect would fall into his tea, would have to be fished out and immediately identified under a lens.

In character he was shy and self-sufficient, but delightful, so I believe, to those who knew him well, keenly humorous, ready to laugh, and laugh at himself. Night after night he would make drawings for his children rather in the manner of Edward Lear, one, for instance, of his small boy on holiday at Charmouth with his toe caught under a gigantic limpet shell; and he was adept at Wiltshire stories. Those who knew him only in his old age and from outside could not have divined the sensibility and gaiety of his inner life, revealed for example in his early diaries, which must be published some day. A diary written on the Riviera and in Italy when he was twenty-five (he had been a naturalist since his school days at Winchester) shifts delightfully from details of a trapdoor spider's nest by his hotel or the thrushes and coots and red-legged partridges on sale in the market to notes on a painting by Mantegna or reading Fergusson on Hindoo and mediaeval architecture, or an account of a ridiculous Englishman off (he was not quite sure which) to shoot moufflon in Corsica or teach horse-racing to Spaniards.

There is no need to end a brief account of this man, whose life was happy and full, by wishing (any more than he would have wished) for some magic means of killing change and stabilizing the past. He knew that much of the business of life lies in contemplation of change and in its digestion. If he realized so much, if he was wise and happy nevertheless, it was largely because he lived upon those roots nourished by the nine generations who had preceded him at Clyffe; and because he was not, like so many of us, homeless at home. So I like to think of him, remarkable and yet a type in the English counties, doing harm to none, neither disorderly in his religion nor a saint, trudging about, knowing every plant for miles around, knowing what the human association had been, century after century, of every house, wall, and corner in two parishes, and collecting into his own garden plants out of a dozen countries.

West of England, 1945

II

SIR JOSHUA REYNOLDS

IMAGINE, IN EIGHTEENTH-CENTURY BREECHES, a not very tall man, inclined to be a little stout, with reddish cheeks, a blunt nose, and a blunt chin, and blunt ears. He has a blunt mouth, with the lower lip rather sparse, and the upper lip partly cut away by an accident, so that it gives him that rather tight look of the straitlaced. Imagine this man looking at you quite actively, but as though you were not a very interesting object. Imagine him handing you, punctiliously, with a well-phrased compliment, in a voice still burred with a Devonshire accent, into a shabby, well-used chair, in a large, well-lighted, well-proportioned painting-room. Imagine that you are an earl, a countess, a Lord Chief Justice, or an actress. Imagine it is 11 o'clock in the morning. The year is 1773, and the man who has just handed you to his painting-chair is getting busy with paint and brushes behind a canvas. You will then be one of the fortunate people who could afford to have their photograph taken, or rather their portrait painted by the eminent Joshua Reynolds.

In 1773 Reynolds was flourishing in the full sunshine. He was fifty. He had just been down to Oxford to get an honorary degree. He had just been made Mayor of Plympton, where he was born. He had been knighted for four years. He had been President of the new Royal Academy for five. He had piled up a fortune. He was friendly with the best men of letters—Dr. Johnson, for instance, and Dr. Goldsmith and Mr. Burke, and Mr. Sheridan and Mr. Sterne—though he was neither so friendly nor so intimate with the best artists.

Unless you had great poise, you would have been rather frightened of Sir Joshua Reynolds. And unless you were astute, his fame as an already Great Master would have deceived you about the kind of man Reynolds was. He was a big man, he was an important man, he was a character; but neither the kind of man nor the kind of artist that I think men and artists ought to be.

Reynolds was exceedingly ambitious. When he was a young man, up from Devonshire, learning to be an artist, he saw Pope in an auction room and managed to shake hands with him; but I am inclined to think Reynolds was impressed, not because the hand he had shaken was the hand of a great poet, but because it was the hand of a famous and, above all, a successful man. Reynolds was not a fool. He must have recognized soon that he was far from being a man of genius. But he lived in the eighteenth century, the century of reason, in which a bishop remarked to Mr. Wesley: 'Enthusiasm, Mr. Wesley, is a very dangerous thing.'

He was never enthusiastic, so far as I know, about anything, either in our sense of enthusiasm or in the more specialized sense in which Mr. Wesley was reproved for the possession of it.

Thomas Edison remarked that 'Genius is one per cent. inspiration and ninety-nine per cent. perspiration'. Reynolds in his own more elegant, eighteenth-century, but none the less spiritually vulgar way, laid it down:

'If you have great talents, industry will improve them: if you have but moderate abilities, industry will supply their deficiency. Nothing is denied to well-directed labour. . . .'

And very little—in his lifetime—was denied to Reynolds. He was industrious. His labour was well directed. He studied the Masters—Rubens, Titian, Raphael, Michelangelo. He worked so hard for forty years that he can hardly ever have seen the outside world. He rose very early and then, according to his biographer Northcote:

'His application to his beloved art was such that he seldom went out of his house in the day time; and if by accident any circumstance obliged him to walk in the streets, it seemed so strange to him, that, according to his own expression, he felt as if everybody was looking at him.'

When could he have found time to refresh his eyes, as good and passionate artists have to refresh their eyes, with constant examination of light, shadow, colours, contours, and objects? He painted all day and amused himself with whist and talk and high life when it was too dark for him to paint any longer.

Sir Joshua lived in a generalizing age. It was the age, I suppose, above others, in which it would have been most possible for a blind man to be a good artist. True to its teaching, he was against details. He aimed at ideal perfection and ideal beauty. He told the Academy students that:

'The whole beauty and grandeur of the art consists in being able to get above all singular forms, local customs, particularities, and details of every kind.'

And Nature for Reynolds, as a true eighteenth-century idealist, was not the material nature that we know. It was nature put through a sieve. No doubt there are more ugly faces in the world than nice ones. But Reynolds held that an ugly face was not nature—was not, he said, according to the common course of things. 'Consequently an ugly face is an unnatural face.'

He advised his own pupils to look at the objects they were painting with their eyelids half-closed—'which gives breadth to the object, and subdues all the little unimportant parts'. He knew that the 'grand style', for instance, of Raphael eschewed details for the grand generalization. But you cannot see the general things, you cannot conceive the grand ones—which is where Sir Joshua went wrong so conveniently—unless you have first seen, and seen beyond, or round, all the little unimportant parts he despised. Therein is the deep difference between the painting of Reynolds and the painting of Gainsborough.

Gainsborough, an artist of emotional temperament who felt the tenderness of life, all of which he could express in the graceful bend of a girl's arm, generalized trees and plants and cows and thistles and houses and people; but he had eyes, to begin with. There are two chestnuts which tell you much about Sir Joshua and Gainsborough. Both of them painted the great actress Mrs. Siddons. When Mrs. Siddons sat to Sir Joshua, he led her to the dais and said, in his best eighteenth-century style: 'Madam, ascend your undisputed throne; bestow on me some idea of the Tragic Muse.'

When Gainsborough painted Mrs. Siddons, he was busy on her face, suddenly threw his brush onto the floor and exploded in good plain English: 'Damn the nose, there's no end to it.'

73

In other words, Mrs. Siddons was an idea, a generalization, a tragic muse, to Sir Joshua, who was painting her with his mind, and she was a woman, an object, with an awkwardly long nose, to Gainsborough, who was painting her with his two exceedingly sharp eyes.

Reynolds generalized, not only because it was the eighteenth-century thing to do, and because Raphael—in a very different way—also generalized. It suited him to do so—he had a character precisely fitted to his age, which explains his eminence while the age endured. He generalized so absolutely because he couldn't see, because he couldn't particularize, because he couldn't draw (his drawings—the few he left—are flat, weak, and tedious), because he couldn't enthuse and couldn't feel to the depths, and because he could only substitute thinking for all these activities. Look at any of his pictures, even at so charming a one as the portrait of Nelly O'Brien—it hangs in the Wallace Collection—and see for yourself how frigid and untrue to facts his generalized drapery and generalized trees and generalized faces and hair and bodies really are. And look how flatly he paints. The arms are flat, the fingers are flat, Nelly O'Brien has a flat dog in her arms.

Now Reynolds himself, I believe, was really flat like this, with colour but without light and shade and depth. Even his friends said that his kindness was chilly. Nothing was positive about him. His passions—if that is not too big a word—were well in hand. As he said to his favourite niece—he only wrote to her for her marriage, by the way, when Burke made him sit down and write:

'I am no great professor of love and affection, and therefore I never told you how much I loved you, for fear you should grow saucy upon it.'

This lukewarm bachelor was seldom very pleasant to anyone or very unpleasant, but only, I am pretty sure, because he never cared enough one way or another. He was extremely diplomatic, he always tried to be even and just, but diplomacy, evenness, and justice cannot be held very great virtues when your nature does not tempt you to be undiplomatic, uneven, and unjust. There is a letter he wrote to his sister, who had kept house for him in

Devonshire, and was in some ways an irritating creature. She was dependent on him and so rather at his mercy. He wrote:

'Dear Sister,

I am very much obliged to you for your kind and generous offer in regard to the house at Richmond not only in giving me leave to use it occasionally but even as long as I live provided I will give it you, but as I have no such thoughts at present I can only thank you for your kindness—tho' I am much older than you I am not yet arrived to dotage as you seem to think I am, voluntarily to put myself in the situation of receiving the favour of living in my own house instead of conferring the favour of letting you live in it.

I am your most affectionate Brother

J. Reynolds.

I have enclosed a Bank Bill of ten pounds.'

It is one of the most unpleasant letters I know; in its most provoking sarcastic moderation it is as like Reynolds as Reynolds and his face were alike.

But do not think that Reynolds was a prig—he was not—or even a snob—though he liked ladies and lords, and had eventually seventeen lords in his funeral procession. He did not mind who sat in his painting-chair, demi-mondaine, bishop, duchess, or beggar. He did not mind who it was he entertained at his dinner table. He did not mind getting tipsy—he once reproved Dr. Johnson for drinking eleven cups of tea. Johnson replied: 'Sir, I did not count your glasses of wine, why should you number up my cups of tea?'

He did not mind what he did or what was done as long as no one was offended, and as long as no one came between him and his ambitions. No, he was an egoist. He was an egoist with a vulcanized heart, neither adamant nor soft. He was a negative character, with energy, brains, and an object in life. He was a skilful mediocrity of the highest kind which always goes up.

'I go with the stream', said Reynolds. The English world, elegant and well-to-do, and ignorant of painting, wanted England to be reputed in the arts, it wanted a grand artist, it wanted its face painted by a grand artist, and it wanted a grand academy under royal patronage—and all these things it wished to have or to be done in a reasonable, understandable, gentlemanly way. And really it was fortunate that it possessed someone to do them as well as they were carried through by Reynolds. After all, he had dignity and polish. He did not let things down. Knowing the world, he painted sentimentalities, grandeurs, great ladies, and lovely ladies, with ease, and sometimes with charm, with all the tricks. He could contrive gay and fanciful compositions in colour upon an eclecticism of form. He painted with everything but power and imagination. Did it matter really that he was a fake Old Master, who falsified his books, so to speak, and achieved what looked to be the correct answer without working out the sum? Did it matter really that he took short cuts, and that so many of his pictures, through his career, darkened, faded, cracked, or melted?

Horace Walpole said he ought to be paid by annuities, each annuity to last as long as each picture. The great connoisseur of the time said that his pictures sometimes died before the sitters: but no matter: better, he said, a faded Reynolds, a darkened, cracked, or melted Reynolds than a portrait by anybody else. Salerooms and connoisseurs show the endurance of this exaggeration of his merit. It is true that some people objected in or just after his lifetime to the dogma of his ineffable greatness. And there was Blake, who had the temerity to write in his copy of the 'Discourses' of Sir Joshua Reynolds against that part of the introduction which dealt with Reynolds's death (and the funeral with the seventeen lords):

> When Sir Joshua Reynolds died
> All nature was degraded,
> The King dropp'd a tear into the Queen's ear
> And all his pictures faded.

Blake called him the doll of the connoisseurs—which he remains —and the President of Fools. Blake (who went for Reynolds intemperately in the name of enthusiasm, particulars, and human feeling, much as D. H. Lawrence once went for John Galsworthy) also said:

'The Enquiry in England is not whether a man has Talents and Genius, but whether he is a Passive, a Polite and a Virtuous

Ass and obedient to Noblemen's opinions in Art and Science. If he is, he is a Good Man. If not, he must be starved.'

Reynolds preached that mediocrity could be turned into genius, Blake believed that Academies were formed to preserve mediocrity. The greatest artist is normality in its perfection. Blake was abnormality raised to a splendid height, Reynolds mediocrity raised by his own application and skill into the simulacrum of greatness. But whose humanity was ever greatly enlarged by contemplating his pictures?

West of England, 1939

12

JOHN CONSTABLE

I WONDER IF YOU have felt (if you have visited the Constable exhibition at the Victoria and Albert, or any other Constable exhibition in the last twenty years) 'I have seen all this before'? If you have ever wondered, as I confess I have, whether Constable, after all, was a great painter?

It is exceedingly difficult to see Constable fairly. We have loved him very much. His way of looking at nature, his way of painting, his out-of-doors quality, have been repeated, without his own original intensity, by innumerable painters, have stared at us from so many walls of so many exhibitions, under so many different signatures. We hear so often that he was a revolutionary, that he was the father of French Impressionism; we know by heart so many of his remarks—'there is room for a natural painture.' And, as a result, our appreciation of Constable is confused. Our sense of what he is, what he remains, is confused by our knowledge of Constable in the history of art.

I don't want to go over that history again. But just to see if I can discover what is permanent in Constable, to discover what we can expect to learn, not of history but of life, what we can gain and feel, from looking at his pictures—now, when a century of disturbance of values separates ourselves from the conditions in which Constable painted. Let us forget the French. Forget the brown landscapes which Constable replaced with natural green; and look at Constable and see what we can find; also what we cannot find. My short answer is that if we go to the Victoria and Albert and look at the sketches (all too cunningly remounted, and shining out to our eyes under fluorescent lighting) we shall find, precisely, Constable himself. Without knowing it, Constable painted himself. I see most of his landscapes as a series of self-portraits, as paintings of Constable's own moods, desires, and disturbances. And I would maintain that Constable mastered the handling of paint far more than he ever mastered himself and his own impulse to paint.

For all his earnestness, and strength of common sense, all his determination to paint in his own way, whatever patrons, public, critics, artists, and the Royal Academy might think, Constable was nervously and delicately sensitive; and I should not say that he was happy. He was not poor. He had not to struggle to keep his children alive, or make a compromise between what he wanted to paint and what he was expected to paint. But inside himself, inside his firmness and his common sense, he was always ill at ease, always in a whirl of emotion. He admires a favourite Dutch picture because he says it is 'still, mild and tranquil'. When he was busy on the pictures he was sending to Paris he wrote: 'One of the largest is quite complete and is my best in sparkle with repose' —with repose—'which is my struggle just now'. At a time of depression in 1834 he wrote: 'Every gleam of sunshine is withdrawn from me, in the art at least. Can it be wondered at, then, that I paint continual storms: "Tempest o'er tempest roll'd"?'

His common sense, and this yearning for repose, kept him from extravagant painting of the mighty forces of nature. There is a good piece about that in Leslie's *Life of Constable*, when he was 'speaking of the taste for the *prodigious* and the *astounding* in art, a taste very contrary to his own', and he used a quotation from the First Book of Kings:

'A great and strong wind rent the mountains, and brake in pieces the rocks before the Lord; but the Lord was not in the wind; and after the wind an earthquake; but the Lord was not in the earthquake: and after the earthquake a fire; but the Lord was not in the fire: and after the fire *a still small voice*.'

There you are: repose again and stillness; but since, as Constable said, his pictures were his acts, were himself; since, as he said, whenever he sat down to make a sketch from nature the first thing he tried to do was to forget that he had ever seen a picture, the result was that the disturbed self always was breaking in upon that desire for repose. He was always painting a Weymouth Bay where the sky filled up with brown cloudage, a Hadleigh Castle where the sky was agitated with darkness, an Old Sarum or a Hampstead Heath where sheets of rain were falling out of the light and blackness of the sky. 'I have to combat from high quarters,' Constable confessed, 'even from Lawrence, the plausible argument that *subject* makes the picture.' Constable was his own subject. Constable painted himself, willy-nilly, through just as much of nature as painting himself required.

So I see in Constable's painting, in the greenness, the sparkle and the dark, the rain, the freshness, the agitated youthfulness, a very moving autobiography, one which is personal also to ourselves, our own moods and disturbances, our own uneasiness, our own desire for freshness, our own wishes for a repose and a calm sunshine and a still small voice which we cannot compass. I see in Constable that much achievement; and just that much limitation. Now and again in some of his sketches—particularly of cloudscape—he emerges beyond pathos into a diamond moment. But if Constable had been a greater man, I feel that he would have mastered (mastered, not falsified) those elements in his nature, and organized them into greater pictures than any he has ever left to us. To which it is no good replying that Constable was essentially romantic, and that the essence of the romantic was to give expressions of mood, unorganized and without the structure and the harmony of the greater masters before and since. In poetry, concurrently with Constable, Coleridge and Wordsworth were romantics, but were possessed of an intellectual power beside which Constable had only the intellect of a child, working instinctively, and without quite knowing why he worked. Sir Kenneth Clark, who is our greatest authority on Constable, has compared him with Wordsworth; and regretted that Wordsworth did not enjoy a painter who was doing much the same with paint as he did himself with language. But I doubt that Wordsworth and Constable were doing the same thing at all. Wordsworth is grand, and Constable is small and exquisite, because Wordsworth did not just mirror himself in nature—though he came near to it at times—did not just use nature as a means of autobiography. Wordsworth did achieve calmness and repose, did find the calm sunshine of the heart, he did believe there was something in nature outside himself, he did, in contemplating nature, develop not only a serene joy, but, out of that joy, a much more grown-up philosophy; by which we can be satisfied at a much deeper level than we can ever be satisfied by Constable's lovely and uneasy pictures.

Sir Kenneth Clark thinks that 'what prevented the poets and

prophets of the romantic movement from recognizing the greatness of Constable was, simply, that he didn't paint mountains'.
I do not believe that at all. Wordsworth, I suspect, must have
seen and considered Constable's pictures; but, if so, I believe he
must have realized their limitations and their incompleteness by
the greater standards—their limitation, that is, to Constable himself. Goethe, another great romantic self-raised above romantic
weakness, put his finger, I think, on the weakness of Constable
when he was talking about Claude. Claude stood 'to nature in a
double relation'. Claude was both nature's slave and nature's
master: her slave because he had to employ nature to make
himself understood; her master because he subordinated nature
to a well-reasoned inspiration. Constable achieved a mastery—a
limited mastery over nature; but then in turn he was the slave
of his own being. What he lacked was that 'well-reasoned inspiration' or control over himself, that full belief of Wordsworth's
that there was something in life and nature outside himself, and
within his power to express. Constable lacked a philosophy.
And Constable was not mature. And so I find myself looking at
his work, and concluding that he is an exhaustible artist; that he
lacks the inner mysteriousness and meaning of the greater,
inexhaustible masters. The limits to the nourishment we can
get from Constable are the limits of human pathos. As an artist
he speaks only to a circumscribed, limited part of ourselves.

And historically—if I can now mention history—it is not a bit
surprising if younger artists at the present are out of sympathy
with Constable, and underestimate him. They feel the limits of
what can be done with just that amount of generalized nature,
genuine freshness and greenness, which Constable exploited with
so much ability and so much affection.

In all the present disputing about art, we must not think that
Constable's kind of painting is fixed as a standard which is the
be-all and end-all of the artist's attitude to nature. Champions
of what they call 'sanity' in art—I see they have now formed a
Society for Sanity in Art—forget that human sensibility does not
stand still like Mount Everest. When I came out of the recent
exhibition at the National Gallery of that very complete, very
exquisite small master Paul Klee (who had a 'well-reasoned
inspiration'), I realized how there was a nature which the small

master Constable saw and used, and a nature—just as authentic—which Klee saw and used. I could see bits of Klee drawings everywhere in London—for instance in the red circle of a traffic light that flashed on outside the Gallery, in the green arrow, like an arrow in one of his water-colours, which flashed on to guide traffic up Charing Cross Road; I could see Klee drawings in the curliwigs of a lamp-standard and in the scaffolding in Piccadilly Circus, just as I could see behind them an ominous, rainy Constable sky impending over Regent Street. Sanity and civilization have a place for the contradictions—though contradiction is not really the right word—between Claude and Constable and between Constable and Klee—or Picasso, or Matisse. The first condition of sanity is so obviously to use your head and your heart, and your eyes.

Home Service, 1946

13

TURNER

I REMEMBER an English art critic referring to Turner caustically as an 'after-dinner painter', a painter whose pictures were like the easy, talented, popular speeches which acceptable guests throw off with the brandy. And I remember also talking about Turner to one of the greatest, if not the greatest, living artists in England, who said, 'look at Turner's scale, look at his size, look at his energy', and who maintained that Turner easily tops any English artist there has ever been. In his long life—he lived till he was over seventy and did not die until the time of the Pre-Raphaelites in 1851, less than a hundred years ago—he worked and painted with fantastic determination. A complete catalogue of Turner's work, from oil to water-colour, would make a thick volume. He painted from boyhood till old age. Such a prodigious performer cannot be rubbed out with the phrase an 'after-dinner painter'.

In fact, if you dismiss Turner, you dismiss (which is a risky thing to do) the whole of the romantic movement in English painting, all of that great outburst of coloured emotion which was spanned by Turner's lifetime. It is another thing to say—I would be inclined to say it without hesitation—that the romantic point of view was not the noblest conception of art which has been evolved and acted upon. But the test of an individual artist is not whether he obeys the spirit of his time—he cannot very well help obeying it; the test is how far he passes beyond it, how far, with its inescapable influence, he discovers himself, discovers the peculiarity of his power, and arrives at last at some universality. Some time ago, talking about John Constable, who was only a year younger than Turner, I suggested that Constable epitomized romantic individualism: I suggested that his pictures were personal, too personal, were an autobiography, were too simply a reflection, a projection of his own personality in terms of one facet of his age. Turner strikes me as the greater man, because his best paintings push beyond individualism, because they reflect not merely Turner, not merely himself, not merely the whole revolutionary age in which he lived, but achieve a validity which appears universal. The flame of Turner's colour expresses a grandiose conception of man as something equivalent to the mighty powers of nature, nature immense and violent. Constable liked the quietness, the still small voice of nature. He liked the nature of green fields and water which was still or slow. He went on one occasion in his life to the English lakes, and found himself unhappy among their wild mountain scenery. Turner exulted in whatever wildness he could discover, the wildness of Wales, the Lakes, Scotland, the Alps, rock, avalanche, waterfall, fire, melted iron, and the enormity of the sea; and at his finest, he was equal to his subject matter. He could, when he wished, be serene and quiet; he could be tempestuous and huge. If a given piece of landscape was too tame, he would bring it up to the height of that tempestuousness he believed in, by ruthless exaggeration. When I say that, I think of one of his drawings of a waterfall in a limestone wilderness of England. It is the peculiar fall of Weathercote Cave. A funnel goes down into the ground. Out of the side of the funnel breaks a river; it thunders down, and disappears from sight in the subterranean darkness of the rock. Turner did two versions of the scene. One is objective and accurate. The stream, the river, emerges and disappears. Round about it, in the drawing, one can see only rock and trees, as in fact rock and trees are alone visible. In the other version, the one I am thinking of, the desolation and power of the waterfall and funnel are exaggerated by painting in around them high mountains which are not there. Turner compelled his landscape, Constable, a humbler artist, was compelled by it. Constable would wait for a figure to cross the scene he was painting. If no figure crossed, no figure would be inserted within the picture. Turner's scene had to obey Turner, obey his conception of human grandeur. If it was not grand enough, the grandeur was added.

Now it is proof of Turner's immensity that his best pictures do survive this exaggerating process. Some, it is true, fail theatrically. But all of them would fail that way if Turner had not learned the basic world, the basic nature upon which he erected his vision, if he had not also learned his mere art, his mere vehicle.

Other artists of his time had grandiose visions of the mighty forces of nature without Turner's mastery of the vehicle, without his mastery of the invisible world in its method of working and existence. Their pictures are patently, fatally theatrical. Of one of them, the artist John Martin, who was never afraid to tackle the end of the world, the last day, the gulfs of hell or the plains of heaven, a fellow artist said, with truth, that he could not paint a great toe from nature. Turner could paint toe, or eye, or rock, or plant. And belonging to a time when order was overthrown for emotion, he explored all the intensities and the expressiveness of colour. When Turner was a boy, a leading exponent of eighteenth-century order, controlling though not suppressing the rise of the temperature of the emotions, was the artist Alexander Cozens. Cozens, too, liked the pinnacled structure of mountains, but he would cross them with bars of serene and motionless or slow-moving cloud. In preference to colour, the thrill of blues and reds and chrome yellows, Cozens, obedient to his time, stuck to browns and greys, staining his paper with coffee. A day or two ago I saw what must be among the loveliest of Turner's water-colours—a stretch of beach, beyond it an azure intensity of sea; above the sea, clouds flecked with blue and pink like the sides of a fish. Someone remarked to me, as we looked at it together, that painting could go no nearer to music. That musical colour Turner developed steadily in his old age, combining it still with the enormous fury of the human spirit expressed in natural fury. Here are some of the titles of pictures which he painted as an old man: 'The Burning of the House of Lords and Commons', 'Snow Storm, Avalanche and Inundation', 'Rockets and Blue Lights to warn Steam-boats off Shoal Water', 'Slavers Throwing overboard the Dead and Dying—Typhoon Coming on', 'The Angel Standing in the Sun'. And I might mention particularly the series he painted of whale-ships, dream whale-ships in flaring seas with whales breaking out of the water—pictures, it is worth recalling, which Turner made only a few years before the American writer Herman Melville was busy on *Moby Dick*, that novel of whale, sea, and the enormousness of man. Another pointer to the essence of Turner's art is his admiration of the poetry of Byron. In fact in Byron, Napoleon, and Turner you have three titanic figures who *are* their age.

Constable, and other romantic painters of the English landscape school, are only a part of their age.

Turner, one feels, never painted himself out. He was always, until death nearly, after something; after an ideal something, still beyond his grasp, or something realized in his imagination if not captured on canvas. In his old age, an American journalist was introduced to Turner at a London picture dealer's. Turner, by this time, was a secretive oddity, living, out of sight, in his imagination. To the journalist he appeared at first a 'little insignificant old man with a nose like an eagle's beak, though a second sight showed that his eye, too, was like an eagle's, bright, restless and penetrating'. 'Half awed and half surprised,' the journalist goes on, 'I held out my hand. He put his behind him, regarding me with a humorous malicious look, saying nothing.' 'Confused and not a little mortified' the journalist turned away, walked down the gallery, looked at the pictures, looked at Turner again, when this time, he did thrust forward his hand and they had a conversation. The journalist praised Turner's pictures. Turner grunted and replied that he 'wished they were all put in a blunderbuss and shot off'. As I interpret that story, Turner in his art and ideas had got, so to say, beyond painting. He had come to know himself, his conceptions, his being, his view of life and time, come to regard what he knew as more important than its expression. And it reminds me of an ancient Buddhist account of the preparation and process of painting religious pictures. The preliminary act was a long one of self-purification and of worship. After that, came the mere painting of the concept arrived at in the ceremonial. But the ceremonial, the act of worship, might be enough in itself, and the painting might never follow. So with Turner, in his enormous act of pagan worship. His paintings were short of his imagined reality, and, for all he cared, might as well be fired off from a gun. I know a portrait drawing of Turner, with eyes which already suggest a vision of the imagined reality. It was a drawing, I believe, Turner did not consent to. He disliked being drawn, and the face he showed to the world—when he showed it—was indifferently hard. He once called on Delacroix, in Delacroix's studio in Paris. 'He made only a middling impression on me,' Delacroix recorded in his journal, 'he had the look of an English farmer, black coat of a rather coarse type, thick shoes—and a cold, hard face.' If there was one kind of man more than another before whom Turner would conceal himself, it was another artist.

According to Vasari, Piero di Cosimo in his old age shut himself up, allowed no one to see him, would not have his rooms swept, or allow his garden to be planted, and became so eccentric that nothing could be done with him, living alone, enraged by flies and shadows. Turner's old age was not less remarkable, less mysterious, or less in character. He had painted popular pictures, he had made money, he was famous; but he passed beyond popularity, the wish for money or the wish for fame. If ever a man explored the possibilities of romanticism in art, it was Turner; if ever a painter gave full expression to the violence, excess, and intoxication of romanticism it was Turner. And romanticism, even if it isolated those elements, does contain elements of what is humanly universal and perpetual. Turner, if you like to put it that way, is somewhere nearer to the beginning of that process in history, which in our two enormous disasters of world war has come nearer, if not quite, to its end. In the arts now in England, and I think in Europe, we can at last see the beginnings of a movement towards balance and composure. So we should now prefer a master of balance such as Poussin to a master of the extreme such as Turner; and, more and more, this is going to make it difficult for us to see Turner, to realize the thoroughness and importance of his achievement, to allow that achievement its value—(its value, I mean, in itself, not in its influence upon European painting). For all that, Turner shines out still, and is likely to shine out for some time to come, as the major sun of English painting.

Far Eastern Service, 1946

14

RUSKIN'S 'MODERN PAINTERS'

RUSKIN SAID when he came to the end of *Modern Painters*
—after working on it for seventeen years—that his fame
might have been served better if he had written one volume
and not five. It was teaching rather than fame he had been after;
and no doubt his teaching on the nature and purpose of art might
be more clear to all of us to-day if the immense five volumes had
been concentrated. Our lack of sympathy with Ruskin, our lack
of interest in anything except his peculiarity, his madness, and
his repellent relationship with Mrs. Ruskin, combine with this
great bulk of *Modern Painters* to obscure from us what Ruskin
had to say. In fact Ruskin was finding himself out in the roll of
sentences from the first section of the first chapter of the first
volume to the last section of the last chapter of the fifth. He
explored as he wrote, digging to his most profound conclusions.

We should remember how, at any rate in time, *Modern Painters*
was written. The first volume was published in 1843 when
Ruskin was twenty-four, the second three years later when he
was nearly twenty-seven. In some ways these first two volumes
are the least satisfactory. After 1846, when the second volume
appeared, there comes a long gap. Ten years go by, filled with
further exploration and examination and thought and with other
writing, including *The Stones of Venice*. Then when Ruskin was
a month short of thirty-seven, he brought out that third volume,
which apprehends the essentials and conclusions of his teaching with
maturity and eloquence. The fourth volume came a year later,
and the fifth, after another gap of four years, in the spring of 1860.
He was forty-one when the last wave of eloquence rolled across
the sand. For seventeen years—more than that, since childhood
—Ruskin had read, travelled, looked, thought, drawn, not only
contemplated pictures and buildings, but plunged into natural
history and science, into meteorology and geology, had analysed
for himself skies and clouds and light and shadow and rocks and
mountains and trees and leaves and petals and stigmas. The

energy of this frail man was extreme, derived from one end and concentrated to one end, which was the exposition of the nobility of art.

If Ruskin was wrong, if he committed confusions which are not warranted by the whole arts of mankind, it would still be a monstrous joke were this immense book issuing from all this labour to contain no illuminations, and to have become now only a useless junk-shop of fine writing and dead notions. *Modern Painters* can be treated in that way. It can be used as a pit in which the anthologist picks sparklers out of the mud. But that is no compliment either to Ruskin or mankind.

You may have read R. G. Collingwood's autobiography. Collingwood's father was Ruskin's secretary. No doubt he suffered from too much Ruskin, as one may have suffered in childhood from too many glasses of sanative liquorice powder. For other reasons than that, the philosophy of art he developed was as different from Ruskin's as the canvases of Picasso are different from the canvases of Turner; but it is worth remembering, in the autobiography, Collingwood's declaration that no philosophies are right or final and that the 'wrongness' of philosophies one holds to be wrong is in every way, positive or negative, a help in the formation and perfecting of one's own views. Collingwood, as a man of our time, argued that painting was not visual, that Cézanne (for all his analytic acuity of sight) painted as nearly as possible as a blind man might paint, and that Cézanne was right. Ruskin, the inheritor of the Renaissance and the new science of the natural order, held that painting was absolutely visual. The artist is first of all, he says, a perceiver.

Ruskin was born into the supremacy of landscape, which is the painting, whatever else it may be, of uncontaminated nature; and nature for the artist, he writes in the first volume, 'must be the pure wild volition and energy of creation'. That is what artists must follow, not nature 'subdued to the furrow and cicatriced to the pollard', not nature 'persuaded into proprieties' or 'pampered into diseases'. He derives in this, as in so much else, from the 'primitiveness' of the eighteenth century. For him nature and art are indissoluble and 'he who walks humbly with nature will seldom be in danger of losing sight of art'. So in the first volume, and especially in the preface to the second edition a year later, Ruskin at twenty-four and twenty-five dogmatizes severely on the artist's duty towards nature and severely reproves the artists of times past for their neglect of nature (though he might have reflected that they had lived before the development of the natural sciences, before men had begun to concern themselves with the accuracies of observation). It is easy to laugh at Ruskin reproving Rubens for his indifference to the proper colours of the rainbow, to laugh at him because he insisted upon meteorologic and geologic accuracies, or because he declared against the painter of antiquity and the mannerists who followed him, that the painter's evil had been 'taking upon him to modify God's works at his pleasure, casting the shadow of himself on all he sees, constituting himself arbiter where it is honour to be a disciple, and exhibiting his ingenuity by the attainment of combinations whose highest praise is that they are impossible'.

There may be those who attempt *Modern Painters* and get no further, and take away the notion that Ruskin was nothing more than the protagonist of the natural accuracies of the Pre-Raphaelite painters. But even in the first volume one begins to see that nature for Ruskin is the beginning, not the end, of a landscape. The painter must love what he sees and will only paint well out of love. Detail must not be sought for the sake of detail, but referred to the great end of painting. It is not 'the calculable bricks of the Dutch house-painters' which constitute great art. Indeed, he puts the whip round the Lower Dutch schools, objects to their display of 'manual dexterities', holds their effect on the public mind to be 'totally evil', and exclaims that 'the best patronage that any monarch could possibly bestow upon the art would be to collect the whole body of them into one gallery and burn it to the ground'. He goes for Dürer, reproves him for 'a morbid habit of mind' which seems 'to lose sight of the balance and relations of things, so as to become intense in trifles, gloomily minute'.

Bit by bit Ruskin's moral and religious as well as aesthetic idea of art begins to appear. His aim is 'to attach to the artist the responsibility of the preacher'. Switzerland, the Swiss mountains, should encourage the painting of the ideal, but 'We do not want *châlets* and three-legged stools, cow-bells and buttermilk. We want the pure and holy hills, treated as a link between heaven and earth.' So, obviously, aesthetics are not enough, nor accuracy, so far as truth (one of his most frequent words) consists of accuracy; and one comes to the shorter volume two in which Ruskin treats of the 'imaginative and theoretic faculties'—theoretic being a term he prefers to aesthetic. Men may have acute perceptions of the beautiful, yet make no right use of them from the corruption of their hearts. He enlarges on the point that, in his view, impressions of beauty are not sensual, and not intellectual, but moral; that is to say, they depend 'on a pure, right, and open state of the heart'. And imagination 'is no small degree dependent on acuteness of moral emotion'.

What this means is clearer from the way Ruskin defines imagination. A very great work of art does not merely transcribe from the sources of beauty in external nature: the mind reflects on them and modifies them and colours them. 'This modification is the Work of Imagination.' Nature is behind each faculty. It is the source of aesthetic pleasures, and so of moral emotion; the aesthetic faculty and the moral faculty, and so of the faculty of imagination. The imagination needs the constant sustenance of external nature, and Ruskin observes that 'many painters of powerful mind have been lost to the world by their suffering the restless writhing of their imagination in its cage to take the place of its healthy and exulting activity in the fields of nature'.

Whatever our estimate may be of this morality of art, of what one of Ruskin's continental critics and admirers has called his 'portentious confusion of aesthetic and moral sensibility', which was his manner of justifying mediaeval art, it is true (whether we like it or not) that works of art do have a moral effect. And whether aesthetics, moral beauty, and imagination are all so linked and dependent on external nature or not, at least Ruskin's conception of art, so far, has a dignity absent from hedonistic notions, which are common enough now, that the core of art is the aesthetic 'thrill'.

So far Ruskin is still the young, rather cocksure, but greatly gifted and, in some ways, penetrative critic of his twenties. After volume two came that gap of ten years before the mature volume of 1856, volume three, in which it is most important of all to read the tenth chapter 'Of the Use of Pictures'. Ruskin's artist may be the perceiver, but he allows also for the inner perception, even if Ruskin would not have gone so far as the painter de Chirico in remarking that what he saw with his eyes open was important, but that what he saw with his eyes shut was more important still. In the more literal sense there is an inner and outer perception, what Ruskin calls the 'cheap deceptive resemblance' to nature, and the 'precious non-deceptive resemblance'. It involves him, but that is by the way, in comparing Constable and Turner; Constable perceives that the grass is wet, the meadows flat, and the boughs shady—'about as much as, I suppose, might in general be apprehended, between them, by an intelligent fawn and a skylark,'—whereas 'Turner perceives at a glance the whole sum of visible truth open to human intelligence'. This may be, as so much of *Modern Painters* is throughout, great exaggeration of Turner's insight and achievement, though, to the reader, Turner is neither here nor there in extracting from the five volumes what Ruskin had to give most notably to the understanding of art. One may as well say, though, that we have the habit of underestimating Turner and overestimating Constable, because one was complex, the other less complex, one full of tricks and expansion, the other restricted and more constantly straightforward. Turner's valuation may still suffer from Ruskin's praise, but I should say that his occasional criticisms of Constable, by no means entirely adverse, are more just than is usually allowed.

Ruskin soon goes on to a deeper idea of inner perception when he remarks that while 'as it penetrates into the nature of things, the imagination is pre-eminently a beholder of things, *as* they *are*, it is, in its creative function, an eminent beholder of things *when* and *where* they are NOT'. So that it is as well not always to put the 'real object' in front of the imagination, because the imagination would think more of the thing if it could not see it.

Behind the detail, then, Turner is no literalist or naturalist, however much he overworks the part of nature; and when he comes to define great art and the great artist the accidents and overweightedness disappear in a lofty and a respectable, if not in the absolute an acceptable, idealism. He concludes that the noblest pictures are 'the result of all the highest powers of the imagination, engaged in the discovery and apprehension of the purest truths, and having so arranged them as best to show their preciousness and exalt their clearness'. This is the greatest art, and the lowest imitates it in 'the subordination of nothing to nothing; the elaborate arrangement of sightlessness and emptiness, the order which has no object; the unity which has no life, and the law which has no love; the light which has nothing to illumine, and the shadow which has nothing to relieve'. He has at this point the splendid phrase that the unity of the noblest pictures issues from 'the magnificence of tone in the perfect mind'.

However much we may subtract of all those opinions which are due to the various accidents of time, and the stress of that time on nature, however much we may shy at in Ruskin's morality, however we may be inclined to replace his view of art as revealing what is God-given (remember those Swiss Alps as the 'pure and holy hills' linking heaven and earth) by a view of art as something which reveals what is most excellently human, we have to acknowledge in *Modern Painters* a final sanity and generosity which are by no means dead. It is true that any discussion of composition is overlaid or implicit only through most of the parts and chapters and sections, and that Ruskin reaches it at last in the fifth volume almost as an afterthought. Still, he maintains that he had avoided it 'only because I considered it too great and wonderful for me to deal with'. Composition or formal invention, he wrote, was 'the quality, above all others', which gave him delight in pictures. He spoke of it well as 'intensity of life' and 'intensity of helpfulness', the 'completeness of depending of each part on all the rest'. But if we think of the years and the spirit of the years through which Ruskin lived and wrote, not merely in England, we shall not be surprised that he praised formal invention briefly rather than analysed it at length.

Ruskin had an insular scorn of the French painting of his day. But in spite of the morality and of standing so high in the pulpit above contradiction, in spite of his aspiration to be what one of the Pre-Raphaelites called him, the Pope of Art, his conclusions much resemble those of Baudelaire—especially on feeling and imagination. Baudelaire was the aristocrat, Ruskin in some ways the socialist and democrat of the arts. He tried to unite incompatibles. Baudelaire was the romantic alert to the painting of his time, Ruskin was the romantic justifying himself through the art of the Middle Ages.

We part from Ruskin in emphasizing far less art's visual nature so as to admit far more, originating in diverse cultures, within the many-acred circumference of art. Remembering that, I can more safely quote from the passage on the function of the artist (which comes from *The Stones of Venice*, written though it was within the temporal and spiritual orbit of *Modern Painters*):

'The whole function of the artist in the world is to be a seeing and feeling creature; to be an instrument of such tenderness and sensitiveness, that no shadow, no hue, no line, no instantaneous and evanescent expression of the visible things around him, nor of any of the emotions which they are capable of conveying to the spirit which has been given him, shall either be left unrecorded, or fade from the book of record. It is not his business to think, to judge, to argue, or to know. His place is neither in the closet, nor on the bench, nor at the bar, nor in the library. They are for other men and other work. He may think, in a by-way; reason, now and then, when he has nothing better to do; know such fragments of knowledge as he can gather without stooping or reach without pains; but none of these things are to be his care. The work of his life is to be two-fold only; to see, to feel.'

Third Programme, 1950

15

ALFRED STEVENS AND THE CAT

IF YOU walk down Chancery Lane, in London, you come at the Fleet Street end to the building of the Law Society. There is an iron fence outside the building, and on each upright of the fence is perched a gilt lion, the 'lion sejant' designed in 1852 by the Dorset-born artist, Alfred Stevens. I walked past the Law Society once, and noticed one of the lions calmly smoking a cigarette which someone had pushed without reverence into its mouth. I should call it an unconscious criticism. Perhaps that someone had been struck by the curious, comic balancing act the lions perform—four feet tucked close together, as though they might fall off at any minute. As Stevens's earliest biographer remarks, his problem in designing the lion (for which the model was a domestic cat) was 'the smallness of the place on which the lion was to sit'.

Stevens—Stevens and the cat—indicate very usefully the nature of art. If you have an academic mind you may call him a 'genius'; you may even, like Mr. D. S. MacColl, call him a master—even *the* Master. If you are not academical, you may call him an eclectic, a mannerist, a craftsman, anything but a true artist who fed upon life. The father of Alfred Stevens was a house decorator, carpenter, and odd-job man at Blandford, where he was born. He was double Dorset, because his mother was a farmer's daughter from the neighbourhood. When Stevens showed signs of becoming an artist, the rector of Blandford St. Mary cast about for some way in which the boy could be trained. The first idea was to apprentice him to Landseer the animal painter. Landseer was too expensive. He wanted a premium of £500. Instead of £500, the rector gave Stevens £50, friends made it up to £60, and with this he was sent to Italy, when he was sixteen years old, in 1833; and he came back to Dorset, without a penny, when he was twenty-five—nine years later. Probably it was the worst thing which could have been done for a talented boy. It was like sending an embryo Darwin to a backward fundamentalist university in Dakota, a boy, moreover, who came from the working class, had little education, was an empty vessel to be filled, and was ready to accept in his most impressionable time all the views of those who had authority of education, knowledge, and position. There is no doubt at all about the talent, but in London he might have developed without perverting himself. He could have had worse teachers than Landseer and he would have been among young artists of his own generation. If he had gone to Paris (impossible in the English spirit of the time), he might have come in contact with such men as Delacroix. With Delacroix it was a maxim, a creed, that 'style depends absolutely and solely upon the free and original expression of each painter's peculiar qualities'—which was just the one thing Stevens never knew, the one thing he would never find out in Rome; and never found out indeed after his return. In his innocence, Mr. Best, the rector of Blandford St. Mary, was to blame. He seems, this local cleric, to have been a connoisseur; and connoisseurs are usually out of date, and out of touch with the living art of their times. Perhaps, too, in the classically rebuilt town of Blandford the eighteenth century was still tenaciously alive. The idea that a young artist must go to Italy belonged more to the eighteenth century than to the nineteenth.

Stevens spent his nine years in Rome, Naples, Florence, Milan, Venice. He copied and copied. He came to know all the Renaissance monuments, the paintings, the frescoes of Italy. It was by copying for the dealers that he kept himself alive; and out of date once more, he finished up by working for an artist of an earlier generation, the famous elderly sculptor Thorvaldsen, who purveyed a soft neo-classicism in white marble. When old Thorvaldsen left Rome to go back to Denmark, Stevens returned to England, twenty-five years old, soaked through and through, in a country which would soon be turning to the realism of the Pre-Raphaelites, with Raphael, Andrea del Sarto, and Michelangelo. He came back when Turner's example (Turner still had nine years to live) and Constable's were helping to revolutionize French painting; and here he was, pickled as deeply in classicism and the antique and the Renaissance as any artist of eighty years before—any artist of the generation whose ideas Turner and Constable had rejected. Perhaps it was the most pathetic perversion of an artist in the whole history of English art.

Stevens stayed at Blandford for a couple of years; he borrowed —this time—another fifty pounds, and went off to London. Then, for a short period, he became what he called a 'Professor of everything' at the new Government School of Design, teaching students and rebelling against 'the meddlesome supervision of ignorant government clerks'. From the time he resigned until he died in 1875, he did everything. He drew, he made sculpture, he painted a few pictures, he decorated drawing-rooms, designed stoves, fenders, daggers for the South American export trade, vases, dessert plates, a figurehead for a yacht and a royal railway carriage for the King of Denmark. The climax—also the disturbance and the trial of his last years—was designing the memorial to Wellington which you can go and inspect in St. Paul's Cathedral.

The Wellington Memorial had been open to universal competition, and Stevens's design (though he was not a prominent artist) had been chosen. The competition was in 1856. When he died in 1875, nineteen years later, the memorial was still incomplete. He delayed, he had many difficulties, he had other work in hand, he would not answer letters of complaint and enquiry from the Secretary of the Office of Works; and not liking officials, he would not let them into his studio. He was ill, he was racked by headaches, he was attacked by paralysis. Worn out at his death, he was then only fifty-eight years old.

I should say, with Delacroix on my side, and in face of Mr. MacColl, that simply because Alfred Stevens did not derive his art, in its roots, from his own peculiar qualities, nearly everything he did was moribund. There have been many posthumous exhibitions—one lately of a well-chosen collection of his figure drawings, done with delicacy and craftsmanship, in which there is not, to my seeing, a speck or a spark of life. Drawings around all the gallery exactly, cleverly, tediously, and damningly alike. Craftsmanship without fault expended on nothing—except on imitation of Italian masters. Even the motto Alfred Stevens put to the model which won him the Wellington Memorial Competition—even that, the high words 'I know of but one Art', was imitated or borrowed from Michelangelo. His stoves, his fenders, his mantelpieces—they are all borrowed in essence, all fitted, so it appears, to the spirit of the times of the Great Exhibition when the products of industry—including the minds of each industrialist—were being clothed in the habiliments of the Renaissance. Such products recall one sadly to comments made by the French critic Taine on the classical casts, the dinosaurs, and odds and ends in the Crystal Palace. 'In truth,' he wrote, 'Rome enriched herself with these things by conquest, England by industry. Thus it is that at Rome the paintings, the statues, were stolen originals, and the monsters, whether rhinoceroses or lions, were perfectly alive and tore human beings to pieces; whereas here the statues are made of plaster and the monsters of goldbeater's skin. The spectacle is one of the second class, but of the same kind. A Greek would not have regarded it with satisfaction; he would have considered it appropriate to powerful barbarians who, trying to become refined, had utterly failed.'

I can look with most pleasure at the few paintings by Alfred Stevens, when life or living people were thrust before his eye. For example, the well-known portrait of Mrs. Collman, the wife of the friend who finally acted as intermediary between Stevens and the Government in the difficult affair of the Wellington Memorial. Yet even in this famous National Gallery portrait there is a chilliness of empty perfection, too much academy, too little Stevens. When he was fourteen, he had painted himself, at Blandford; and that early self-portrait (now in the Tate Gallery), dramatically done, simplified, with its full mouth, its shining eyes, and dark hair, possesses, in spite of the naïvety and 'primitivism' of the untrained artist, something personal and peculiar, a strength, a genuineness, a suggestion of what might have become of Stevens if he had been tougher in mind and if his childhood as an artist had not been smothered and smoothed by Italy. The same might be said of an early, terse portrait of that Dorset clergyman who sent him there.

Much about Stevens himself was attractive. He was fastidious. He thought highly and earnestly of the duties of being an artist; he worked, and he had determination. He was solitary and independent. Truly academic, he did not like academies. The President of the Royal Academy suggested that he should submit his name for election. He replied that he did not believe in the

Academy. To the Academy which had refused a drawing he submitted in 1852, he never sent another thing; never, the most academic of all English artists except Reynolds or Leighton, exhibited at the Academy once in his lifetime. One cannot help sympathizing, too, with his attitude towards interfering officials, and his refusal to answer their letters if he felt the letters interfered. All of this at a time when artists were more than usually obsequious, and anxious to be in the swim, to have R.A. after their names, and to possess a butler and a coachman.

A solitary, who never married and kept peculiar pets (such as a sparrow hawk), he seems to have been generous, friendly, and helpful, to have been much liked by students and to have won devotion from his few friends. His smile was winning, his voice unusually sweet. A mature self-portrait of him in a velvet coat certainly shows you an earnest, handsome man, sensitive (to art, if not to life), with generous features and rich, untidy hair. Alfred Stevens is a Victorian. A great many Victorians show their distinction of time by a fundamental—a total—self-deception; by expending great talents in doing big things ill, by spending themselves in belonging to anything except their own century, by deriving their art, whether painting or sculpture or architecture or writing, from times past. If the artistic language of an age is obsolete, if it is not the way of seeing which is properly current in one's age, then however skilfully it is used, however skilfully the pictures are painted or the drawings drawn, however much academic perfection is achieved, the paintings and drawings will soon appear false and empty. So it has been with nearly all the work of Alfred Stevens. A gentility intervenes. It is curious to think that the great Courbet, that ungenteel, powerful, sweaty interpreter of men and women, still life, landscape, rock, wave, stream, and tree, that very real artist whose work seems timelessly alive, was only two years younger than Stevens. Courbet had no use for idealism. 'Paint angels? I have never seen angels. I cannot paint what I have never seen.' An extreme statement, but for the time one which promised health and achievement. Courbet did paint what he saw, heightening the language somewhat in his own peculiarity. We still look at his paintings, enjoy them, and realize their 'truth'. And Courbet powerfully affected the art of his successors. The authentic stream of European art flows through him. To Alfred Stevens an angel or a cherub was something he had seen—in other men's work; and he could reproduce their angels and cherubs, for manufacturers to copy *ad nauseam* in bronze, with that inappropriateness and pride which seems to us so vulgar in Victorian ornament. The stream of European art avoided him; and the lifeless can have no influence upon subsequent life. When Courbet occupied himself with what he saw, a wave or a limestone crag, Stevens was busy with decorative allegories of Temperance and Truth, History and Arithmetic. Translated, Courbet says 'Here is something I must paint', Stevens says 'I have an allegorical idea. Fashioned by my good taste, it will elevate the people.' In the year Courbet painted a strange and powerful design out of the contortion of two wrestlers on a field, Stevens was busy with that comic lion and 'the smallness of the place it was to sit on', that lion not quite out of the circus, not quite out of heraldry, not quite the cat, and not at all out of the strange Africa of the mind. It deserved the cigarette end.

West of England, 1946

16

HOW TO LOOK AT AN
ART GALLERY

THE FIRST PICTURE I ever bought came from a jeweller's shop at Looe in Cornwall. I was eighteen or nineteen at the time, I was just going up to the university and thought I had better buy something to hang in my rooms. So down I went to this jeweller's shop, where painters of picturesque Cornwall exhibited things they could never get into the Academy. There I bought a wishy-washy landscape in water-colour of Cornish fields and a coloured engraving of pilgrims on the Pilgrims' Way, trudging to Canterbury between black yew trees under a sickle moon in a green sky.

I remember being rather dashed when my tutor came in to see me when I had flu. He looked at the engraving over the mantel-piece and remarked (he was a mediaevalist and an historian) that pilgrims did not use the Pilgrims' Way, and instead of walking at night-time would have been in the nearest inn, drinking ale.

But I did not look at those two works of frail art very much, and I do not think I went to art galleries very often until I started to work in London. Then it was the Tate Gallery I went to chiefly. At Oxford I had picked up odds and ends of knowledge about Cézanne and a stranger artist named Picasso; and I started going to the Tate—I may confess it—because I met people who talked with ease about Picasso, Cézanne and Seurat and Van Gogh, and I wanted to talk about them as well. If I liked paintings such as Van Gogh's 'Yellow Chair', it was in a vague way. I could get along without pictures as easily as I could exist without champagne or Turkish baths.

But sometimes, when I happened to be near Trafalgar Square, I used to climb into the National Gallery. There I found one picture I did like, and which began to get hold of me very strongly indeed. It was Titian's 'Bacchus and Ariadne'. I liked it first of all because it was so near one of my favourite poems—Ariadne's song in Keats's *Endymion*. And it so happens that the 'Bacchus and Ariadne' is one of the great pictures you can begin to like before you know why or before you know anything much about painting or painters. For a long time the 'Bacchus and Ariadne' was the only thing I really looked at in the National Gallery for twenty minutes or half an hour at a time, absorbed in its harmony of shapes, its blue and tawny colours, and letting my interest always come back to the pattern of stars in full blueness of the sky.

Then one day the art critic of the paper I worked on in Fleet Street asked me if I would come round the shows in Bond Street with him; I was flattered by the invitation; and so I began to find my way regularly to art exhibitions; I began pretty regularly to see paintings by modern European masters—de Chirico, Picasso, Matisse, Braque, and so on. I began to find myself remembering certain pictures, and being reminded of them by things I saw—women in public houses, or patches of peculiar blue in the sky, or the rain-smoothed yellow of a sandpit on Hampstead Heath, or the curious way in which the wind moves the long, thin leaves of a willow tree.

I began to find that pictures were a necessity. Two things I read influenced me—one was Leslie's *Life of Constable*, and the other was an essay in a paper called 'The Tyro' by Wyndham Lewis. You may know in the first room in the National Gallery on the left of the stairs, a solemn and, I think, an intensely captivating landscape by Poussin [1]—a landscape with deep green trees, and glimpses of an extraordinary dark and luminous blue sky between white stacks of cloud. I found that Constable knew this picture very well and talked of its grave moral feeling; and then in a lecture Constable talked about Claude (Claude was a painter I had hardly begun to look at or like). 'In Claude's landscape all is lovely'—this is what Constable said—'all amiable —all is amenity and repose; the calm sunshine of the heart'. And I began to look at Claude, I began to look in his pictures at the National Gallery for precisely that calm sunshine of the heart, which was a sunshine I was needing at times very much. I was beginning to understand that pictures were continually—if it doesn't sound a bit priggish to say so—a part of life. And then,

[1] Or attributed to Poussin.

as I say, I read that essay by Wyndham Lewis, and found there clearly and persuasively explained just what I was half feeling and groping for.

Lewis declared that painting is 'an account of life'. To begin with, he said, 'the work of art exists in the body of the movement of life, and when we are speaking of art we suddenly find that we are talking of life all the time'.

My eyes were really opening at last. I could begin sweeping my mind clear of the dust of a too eclectic nonsense about 'significant form'. I was beginning to enjoy pictures knowing *why* I was enjoying them.

I selected fewer pictures in art galleries and I was looking at them more intently. At the same time, by examining myself I could see which paintings I liked just because they satisfied certain peculiarities of my own make-up, and touched on certain associations which were pleasant or fascinating to me. I was beginning to distinguish such 'personal' paintings from paintings, in an ordinary phrase, which carry one out of oneself. So, by going to art galleries, I was learning a great deal, not just about art, but about myself, and about the life and nature of human beings. I was also enjoying all the physiological, sensual pleasure you get from rhythms of line, form, and colour.

So I am fairly sure that the first rule about art galleries is to remember that when you are looking at pictures you are looking at life all the time. If you do not feel that, or if you do not feel you ever can feel it, there is not much point in going inside a gallery. Art galleries are not very pleasant places as a rule— except for the pictures. The floors are hard, over-polished, and tiring. The lighting is usually disgraceful, and nine times out of ten the pictures have glass in front of them, so that instead of a masterpiece, you see at first your own collar and tie and the reddish end of your nose. My other rules are: Look at what you like, but find out why you like it, and do not make the mistake of thinking that what you like is the best, or that what you do not like is bad.

Do not look at too much, especially if there are great pictures by great painters in the gallery you are visiting. A great painting may have as much in it as a great novel five hundred pages long. When you visit a gallery for the first time, you are perfectly justified in carrying away an impression of only one or two or three pictures. When I went to Munich to see the Alte Pina-kothek—and I visited it seven or eight times—I carried away a strong impression of only three paintings—Goya's 'Turkey-cock', Claude's 'Hagar and Ishmael in the Desert', and Altdorfer's 'St. George'—but I think the impressions of the trio justified the return fare from Victoria.

And do, if you can afford it, buy photographs of the paintings you like. Lively experiences grow dull. Photographs help to keep them lively; and it is surprising how much you did not really notice in the gallery you can learn afterwards from a photograph.

My last rule is give yourself a rest from masterpieces. And that brings me to local galleries. There is not the slightest reason why one should look down on local galleries because most of the masterpieces happen to be corralled in Trafalgar Square, or the Tate Gallery, or the Wallace Collection.

In the typical Corporation Art Gallery, there is always an acreage of rubbish, but I am inclined to agree with an artist I know who says that bad paintings should be preserved as well as good ones. They are extremely helpful as pointers to the good. And they tell you a great many fascinating things about human beings, fashions, and failings.

But there is nearly always something worth seeing in the Corporation Art Gallery besides the bad pictures. Good painters are not painting masterpieces all the time, and I would go into any gallery on the chance of finding an attractive picture by some-one I had never heard of, or a sketch or drawing by a master or out of a master's studio, or an early water-colour by Cotman or Bonington or Cornelius Varley, or a naïve painting by some untrained artist. I remember some surprises of that kind—going into Glasgow Art Gallery on a black, greasy, bitter, cold-watery Glasgow day, and being bored to death by inferior copy after copy. Then I turned a corner and found a delightful and entirely unexpected painting by Watteau, not one of his delicious assemblies of elegant ladies and their lovers and their lutes under elegant trees, but a painting of troops bivouacking under an ominous brown sky. I remember walking out of the fierce heat of a very suburban lane in Split in Yugoslavia into a tiny art gallery, in which there were three fine, savage, satirical drawings by George Grosz, one of the artists, I suppose, least approved of by Hitler and one of the most inventive of all German draughts-men. I might have heard of Grosz at the time. I had never before seen anything by him, so that chance encounter in a Dalmatian town woke me up to enquire into his work and collect the books in which his drawings are reproduced. By contrast I went once into the museum at Swindon, that most dismal of southern towns; and I found there a water-colour of Swindon bridges. It was naïve, it was amateur; also, it was a subtle, intricate knitting of shapes; and for a long time it seemed to me the only respectable work of the human spirit which could be observed in all of Swindon.

There are, I believe, more provincial art galleries in Great Britain than in any other country of Europe or the world. They have the worst of names, and on the whole they deserve it. But I hope before I die to go into every one of them, from Aberdeen to Truro and Belfast to Brighton (in which art gallery, by the way, inside the Royal Pavilion, you will see a miracle of pictorial drama, 'The Raising of Lazarus', by Jan Lievens).

West of England, 1938

17

THE MUSÉE WIERTZ, OR THE
USES OF BAD ART

I SUPPOSE it would be reasonable to say there are so many
good pictures in Europe and so little time in life to see them
that there is no point in going to enjoy pictures such as you
will find in the Musée Wiertz in Brussels. Excuses could be made.
For instance, that bad painting illuminates the good, that from
these bad as well as from the good you can discover the mental
climate of an age. It depends on your digestion. I myself should
delight in a book on the great bad painters of the nineteenth
century, on the egoism of such men as Wiertz, and Leighton, and
Watts, and Sidney Cooper, preserved intact for us in special
museums. By going to the museums or galleries we can at least
learn about human beings as some of them were in one of the
strangest of centuries. Wiertz is more fascinating than any of
these bad painters I have mentioned; and you will find the horrors
he painted in the corner of a pleasant, bosky street in Brussels,
near the Natural History Museum. In the vulgarest shape
Antoine Wiertz was the Romantic Hero devoted to art, the hero
and the victim of his own epic, the man—the Byronic man—who
would not compromise and forced Belgian society to accept him
as the hero he made of himself, indeed to build him the studio in
which his enormous pictures are preserved, more or less, in their
decay.

He was born, as you might expect, in 1806, so he was a little
younger than Géricault, Delacroix, or Delaroche. His father had
been a soldier in Napoleon's armies, his mother was a Walloon;
and both these parents were uneducated. There is always a
hagiographical story in painters' lives about the discovery of
their genius. Someone came into the Wiertz household and
recoiled from a frog lying on the hearth. 'It's nothing,' said Mme
Wiertz. 'Only a toy Antoine has carved with his pocket-knife.'
The story got about, the boy acquired a patron, and was trained

as an artist. His father filled him with ideas about glory. He studied in Paris and in Rome. His egoism began to swell and he set himself an aim typical of the period: he must paint canvases as large or larger, as great or greater, than any by Rubens. There is another story. As a young man—Belgium then was still ruled by the Dutch—Wiertz was in the museum at Antwerp one day when the Prince of Orange walked around. Wiertz pretended not to see him. The painter whose student he was protested about his bad manners. Wiertz replied, 'Why should I take my hat off to that fellow when'—pointing to the pictures by Rubens—'I've never taken it off to this one?'

It was Thorwaldsen, the Danish sculptor in Rome, who first praised Wiertz. Thorwaldsen looked at his first large painting, 'The Greeks and the Trojans disputing over the Body of Patroclus', and said, 'This young man is a giant'; which was no news to Wiertz. He wanted to exhibit the picture in the Salon, in Paris. The picture was held up on the way and arrived too late, the authorities would make no exception, and that was that. The giant was outraged, he pronounced 'Portraits for soup, pictures for glory'. Portraits would keep him alive and pay for the paints, the canvases, the stretchers, and the frames of eternal glory. The glorious pictures he would refuse always to sell. Like Benjamin Robert Haydon in London, Wiertz had difficulty in finding space which was long enough and lofty enough for painting immensities. In Liége, in 1840, he managed to get hold of an abandoned church. In the church, by 1842, he had finished 'The Revolt of Hell against Heaven', which is almost too tall for the barn of the Musée Wiertz. It is nearly 34 feet high. 'The Revolt' was not for sale; but Wiertz offered it to the cathedral at Antwerp on one condition: it must hang alongside Rubens's triptych of the 'Descent from the Cross' in the south transept. The cathedral had the sense to say no. Observe how Wiertz behaved not only like Benjamin Robert Haydon, or like James Ward who competed against Rubens, but like Turner who competed against Claude, and left two of his pictures to the National Gallery on a condition—which does not seem to be observed at the moment—that they should hang for ever between two paintings by Claude.

Portraits for soup, pictures for glory. Wiertz moved to Brussels and found an empty factory. Perhaps it gave him length rather than height. Here he painted a 'Triumph of Christ', long as the 'Revolt of Hell against Heaven' had been tall. Though Wiertz, I suppose, deceived himself, I cannot help thinking he also calculated the steps to glory. He gave up classical subjects for grandiose religious ones. He proclaimed his poverty and his purpose and his defiance. The 'Triumph of Christ', designed also to be a triumph for Wiertz, was accepted for the Brussels Salon of 1848; but it was too enormous, as Wiertz must have known it would be, to go into the Salon. It was exhibited in the factory. The Russian government offered to buy it for 100,000 francs. The Prince of Prussia (afterwards William I) is said to have offered 300,000 francs. No, it was not for sale. The Belgians were taken in by this mixture of self-deception and calculation.

There are times when society especially needs a hero of art or a hero of letters. It may be a Wiertz, it may be a Rupert Brooke. In 1848, when Wiertz exhibited the 'Triumph of Christ', Belgium was a young country. It was only nine years since Belgian independence had been assured by the Treaty of London. Here, in Brussels, was a Belgian painter who painted big pictures, moral pictures, religious pictures, who was defiant, who talked about glory which was something beyond the notions of a good bourgeois or an honest artisan. He must be as big as his pictures. Wiertz is and must be our hero.

London was more sensible about the claims of Benjamin Robert Haydon, but the situation was not the same; and Wiertz used the situation audaciously, cunningly, impudently. He conceived that the Belgian government might build him a studio big enough for his big pictures, a studio with living-quarters attached. In return he would make over the glorious achievements to the State. It worked. The hero extracted nearly 90,000 francs. The result was the Musée Wiertz, as it became after his death; and we should now go down to the Rue Vauthier, pay for our admission and enter the Barn. Here are the vast canvases, the 'Revolt of Hell', the 'Triumph', on walls from which the distemper is peeling; and many more, the 'Beacon of Golgotha', the 'Lion of Waterloo', 'Napoleon in Hell', 'Human Greed', 'Pride', the 'Last Cannon'—Peace breaking the last cannon in two over the dead of a vast battlefield. Acres, in fact, of sententious violence. Baudelaire was in Brussels in the last years of Wiertz's life and his own. Wiertz seemed to him just the right artist for that Belgian civilization he jeered at, a business civilization of *les Belges*, who blew themselves up with beer and Geneva and sat on their behinds and barked at the moon, vomited like Englishmen, caught pox to imitate the French, jeered at Heaven and believed in progress. It was these sententious pieces which made him write down: 'Wiertz, the great painter around here. Painting in the manner of the Encyclopaedists, philosophic and humanitarian pretensions. Shocking specimen of stupidity and rascality.' They were paintings, so Baudelaire thought, for imitators and counterfeits with a collective mind. I do not know if Baudelaire saw pictures of another kind which now help to fill the Musée Wiertz, though Wiertz apparently exhibited them in his studio. When I was there they had sold out at the desk of post-cards of the 'Premature Burial', which shows a hand coming out of a coffin. That was the kind of thing Wiertz painted once the Belgian government arranged for his comfort and his egoism. Or it was one kind. He painted pictures of a burnt child, a suicide, a mad woman boiling her children, as well as a triptych (more skilful than many of his works) of the 'Thoughts and Visions of a Severed Head', with no pretensions, philosophic or humanitarian. And also a number of overripe nudes, though now and again a moral piece, such as 'The Last Cannon', intervened. Even from the large pictures, Baudelaire must have realized that Wiertz dealt in morbidity and exoticism and was an untalented or journalistic counterpart to his own Delacroix, or to Géricault, or to himself. It was a relation like that of Ann Radcliffe to Blake, or Maturin to De Quincey; or, in English painting, John Martin to Turner.

Where Wiertz betrays his journalism is not only in the poor structure and drawing, in the imitation of more than one current style, in the absence of a style of his own, and in the pretentiousness of his virtue. No, defiant and combative, he was quite ready, at the decisive moment, to accept the francs and the adulation from the good bourgeois. The bourgeois, in the shape of the journalists in Brussels or the Belgian government, had only to say 'Wiertz is glorious', and he would accept the praise of the world he despised and eat his dead dog, off its golden dish, and relapse into being the trivial gory sensationalist which he was in fact all the time. He could not say, even with as much truth as Byron:

> I have not loved the world, nor the world me;
> I have not flattered its rank breath, nor bow'd
> To its idolatries a patient knee,
> Nor coin'd my cheek to smiles, nor cried aloud
> In worship of an echo; in the crowd
> They could not deem me one of such.

There is a little genuine in most counterfeits, a little in Wiertz, who in early life painted a few charming pieces of *genre*; but he was indeed the Romantic pretender, the grandiose liar, he was the shocking example of stupidity and rascality; though, if he had not succeeded, he might also have cut his throat and shot himself like Benjamin Robert Haydon or like the figure in his own picture of the suicide. As it was, he died in his bed of a malignant anthrax in 1865, when he was fifty-nine, ignorant of the mockery of Baudelaire which would also be the judgment of the future.

It may be true Wiertz sacrificed himself to his art, but it was precisely to *his* art. His trouble was lack of talent, and lack of the humility which ought to have gone with his pride. The art was not worth the sacrifice; and it is hard to see a difference between the man like Wiertz and the sharp and not very honest business-man who deals also in good works and is knighted at last for public services. Going around his museum is like going into the hollow of a roc's egg, a little broken, in which the glory has long ago addled and dried up. One has to allow a pathos of decayed vanity. Here, with the dust on them, are Wiertz's flute, hats, medals, spurs, ruler, and tubes of paint and sketch books, in a brown cupboard. 'Pride,' Wiertz has written over the studio, 'the virtue which inspires masterpieces and wounds other men's self-esteem. Modesty, the mask which flatters the self-esteem of other men in order to attract praise.' And look again at the masterpieces, on the damp walls, in a bad condition (one of them has a hole in it), which the State acquired as a bad bargain. Look at 'The Two Girls, or la Belle Rosine', in which *la belle*, naked to the waist, contemplates a skeleton, or at the other pieces of dull pornopicturizing. Look at Wiertz's idea of himself in 1860. He is black-bearded and long-haired, he wears a cloak, his attitude is Byronic, and he looks towards a ladder, leading, I suppose, to the higher reaches of a tall canvas. And then look at the death mask in black bronze on a black velvet plaque, which shows a mean and keen little head.

We must not boast. We have our own Musée Wiertz in the valley at Compton, outside Guildford, filled with the outrageously empty pictures of George Frederick Watts, a better bad painter and a duller man. The one belongs to violent and outrageous romanticism, reflecting feebly the great things of the time, the other belongs to romanticism become senile. One is feebly wild, the other feebly idealistic and conventional. They stand in different settings for two different self-satisfactions. It would have been a terrible, a farcical thing if either Watts or Wiertz could have laid their hearts naked like Baudelaire and then taken a good look.

Third Programme, 1950

18

SQUABBLES ABOUT ART

WE HAVE ENJOYED something in England which we had missed since the war began—a squabble magnificent about the arts. Through the British Council, the French arranged for us, at one of our museums in London, an exhibition of pictures by two of their principal painters, Matisse and Picasso. The exhibition was opened by the French Ambassador. The newspapers at once filled with letters, asking IS THIS ART? The granddaughter of one of the English Pre-Raphaelites protested publicly at the exhibition, and waved an umbrella, because it was not art as her grandfather had understood it (she forgot that still more of a rumpus was made, a hundred years ago, when her grandfather and his friends first exhibited their pictures). Picasso, upon whom the indignation centred, is not a young artist. He is over sixty. His pictures have been familiar in England for thirty years. He had painted steadily on in Paris under the German occupation. For six years we had seen none of his work; we had forgotten its force; and when it did arrive, when Londoners did go to the sedate and sober Victoria and Albert Museum, and when they did examine these violent, big, strong pictures with their elongated, twisted, cruel-seeming bodies in a topsyturvydom of nature, they were puzzled, then afraid, then angry. What the rowdy business boils down to is a squabble between ancient and modern; between the ancient, classical notion that art, to some degree, imitates life, and the modern, revolutionary notion that art is something the artist makes irrespective of its resemblance to things we see. It is something of a world problem, which has not been resolved—yet—for the ordinary man.

Let us go back in England about a hundred and sixty years, which is roughly when modern art—or this modern revolution in the arts—began. Before then, someone who felt that he knew about art, someone who had had an orthodox training in art, would have said two things: first, that the painter was *not* free to paint anything he liked; second, that nature must not only be imitated, but improved upon.

The painter was thought to be a second string to the poet or the historian. His job was thought to be taking a subject from poetry or history or tradition and painting it. His painting had to resemble nature. But the old idea had been that nature, the things we see every day, was imperfect; that the only nature painters could paint was nature-at-its-very-best, or in its state of ideal perfection. If a painter needed to paint a man or a woman, it must be a perfect man or woman; if he needed to put a tree into a picture, it must be the ideal tree of its kind, not the particular tree outside his studio.

Then, about 1780, came the revolution, that revolution we call 'Romantic', which, eventually, brings us down in our own day to Picasso. One of the unwitting pioneers of this revolution, the German-Swiss painter Fuseli, living in England, and a member of the Royal Academy, had lectured to students and told them that artists, whatever the old-fashioned might say, were at last *free* to find subjects for themselves, 'without recourse', Fuseli said, 'to tradition or the stores of history or poetry'. Painters were free to paint what they liked; and they began—this is the point—to paint their own individual moods or feelings. They were not expected any longer to think out all of their picture before they painted it. They began to paint spontaneously; to paint what they—the individual artists—were 'struck with at the first view'. Sixty years before, that would have been blasphemy against the rule and the soul of art.

To express *themselves* spontaneously, they began to paint nature, not according to the old rules of painting an improved nature; they began to paint nature as they saw it. In the old days of rule and tradition, painters had painted *inside* their studios. Now that they had become free of poetry, history, and tradition, they began to paint outside their studios, in the open air. John Constable said that, if he could afford it, he would never paint a landscape 'anywhere but in the open air'. That, too, would have been blasphemy in the days of Constable's grandfather.

With this revolution of individual self-expression through nature, painters had begun to depart from common sense, the sense of things common by the eye to all mankind. In our day,

H   113

what we call modern art has simply carried that process further and further. You will say, 'Your Constables stuck to nature, anyway.' So they did; but self-expression *was* the thing which mattered and, later, artists began to get bored with sticking to nature, and painting it over and over again; they wanted more freedom, and still purer expression of themselves. Thomas Hardy, bored with painters who just turned out these repetitions of nature, explained the situation more than sixty years ago; he said that 'Nature was played out as a Beauty, but not as a mystery'. He did not want to see any more paintings of the 'outside' of nature. 'I want to see the deeper reality underlying the scenic, the expression of what are sometimes called abstract imaginings.'

And it is just these more or less 'abstract imaginings', fifty and sixty years later, that artists of to-day have given us, and which still cause a row.

Let me explain just a bit more why we make a row. In the familiar masterpieces, say by Titian or Vermeer, or Velasquez, there is a great deal more to the picture than the resemblance of the things within it—whether a leopard, or a star, or a tree, or a woman—to leopards, stars, trees, or women in nature. There is the deeper delight of the way the things are coloured, the way the colours make a tune, the way the different lines and different shapes also make a tune. Though tune is rather a small word: I suppose for a great picture, 'symphony' would be nearer the mark. Now the first thing most of us take in when we look at one of these celebrated pictures is its likeness to nature, and the story its women and leopards, and nymphs and goddesses tell us; and the mood of the picture. The last thing we take in is the clever, intricate symphony of colour and shape and line. Many modern artists have tried to take away the things, or to distort the appearance of things; and so to concentrate on the symphony. It is putting the final difficulty, or the final meaning, first; and we dislike it. It is puzzling. I think it does mean an art which is not so rich and so satisfying as the older kinds of art, because it does leave something out. But I also think we, too, should be wearied (even if we were not so puzzled) if art now was simply a moribund imitation of this older art. Yet those of us who are puzzled, expect art to be what Constable and Turner and the rest of them made it when they first revolted; when they began this revolution modern artists have carried, to our bewilderment, so very much further.

There are several other complications, though; and I will mention one. In the modern world you cannot expect art to develop more or less smoothly as it has in the past, one European tradition developing, without too big a jump, out of an earlier European tradition. For this reason: museums, art galleries, the history of art, and anthropologists and archaeologists have, more or less suddenly, made available to us, at one time, all the art traditions of the world, past and present. A modern artist may, and he often does, absorb something from Italian art, African art, Chinese art, ancient Mexican art, Palaeolithic Cave art, and so on, blending them into a personal style of his own. Henry Moore, the English sculptor, owes much, for instance, to ancient Aztec sculptors and to the Italian painter Massacio. The Swiss artist Paul Klee, whose work is being exhibited now in London (and also exciting a fuss), had obviously looked at all manner of art, including the art of the Australian black fellow. This means that modern art has anything but the traditional Western appearance. Perhaps we are seeing the beginning of a new world tradition of art; and for a long time that is bound to look a bit odd, and unfamiliar, and puzzling to most of us within the narrowness of our national inheritance.

Overseas Service, 1946

19
ART FOR EVERYONE

I SUPPOSE the way we are organizing art—'art for everyone'—in Great Britain is part of a belief in democracy. One of our major organizers, Sir Kenneth Clark, stated his own convictions the other day about art for everyone in a message to the people of Swindon, a town which has made remarkable efforts to stimulate music, painting, and drama. Sir Kenneth told Swindon we can only shake off squalor and ugliness 'by the growth, in each individual, of a new feeling for order and beauty'.

So he considers it very important indeed 'that a town like Swindon should be making this great effort to give its citizens a new vision'—by which their lives will be richer. Much the same conviction is behind the work of the Arts Council, the principal organizer of art in Great Britain. The Council believe that the arts 'are not merely a luxury for the rich'. So, with a public grant, the Council go to work through their twelve regions and their Scottish and Welsh offices, to encourage 'art activities' of every kind. They arrange exhibitions, concerts, theatre companies. They work through local centres, art clubs, and music societies. They give concerts in factories, concerts in distant, inaccessible places that hardly ever hear good music. Last year, for instance, the Arts Council sent a concert party out into the Atlantic, in winter, to the Isles of Scilly; the musicians clutching their instruments in the little launch that reels and rolls from island to island; and then, on one of these islands, finding that some two-thirds of the population, on a black tempestuous night, had turned out to hear them play.

The Arts Council believe that the local activities they help to organize will be, in their own words, of undoubted 'value to the future of the arts in this country'. That is where my doubts begin.

I am not sure this is the way to help the 'future of the arts'. When you look round, you find it is the audiences for art, rather than the arts themselves, which are being helped and encouraged.

I want to see the arts—including the artist—*and* the audience equally helped. That needs explanation.

Behind much of this work over here to bring art within everyone's reach, behind its energy and unselfishness, I believe you would discover, in rather a confused form, the teaching of the English sculptor, Eric Gill. Gill preached that there is no distinction between the artist and the ordinary man—or that if we make such a distinction now, it is wrong and false. In fact, Gill believed the artist is not an extraordinary kind of man, but that every man, every one of us, is some special kind of artist. If we all realized it—realized we were artists of some kind or other—we should discover a sympathy for art; what is more important, we should respect art, in other more gifted artists and in ourselves, as a valuable, necessary part of the natural order of our lives.

That wonderful, desirable state of affairs—it cannot be produced by looking, as we do, after 'the future of the arts in this country'. Can we bring it about just by seeing that more people look at more pictures (painted by others), go to more plays and better plays (written by others), hear more music and better music (composed by others), in a factory canteen or on the Scilly Islands? Isn't it possible that all this organization of *art-that-already-exists* is, at any rate for that result, that best possible result, the wrong kind of organization? Or, putting it more generously, only half the right kind of organization?

I could believe in our encouragement of art for everyone, in Great Britain, if it were based more, much more, on the production, the making, of art by artists specially talented and by ourselves. The Arts Council do not entirely neglect this development of art in everyone. They do a little to help the professionals. Yet, practically, the emphasis *is* on spreading the arts ready-made. I cannot see that such action is going to make it easier for the arts to come more and more energetically into our lives.

We have, in the modern world, done that one thing Eric Gill says we ought not to have done: we have come to regard the artist as a different kind of person. Most of us do not want art, at any price. We have made the artist into a type: eccentric, aloof, long-haired—an enemy. We do not like him much—till he is dead. Yet art has existed in nearly all societies we know of. In primitive societies and advanced societies, in prehistory and in history. Why? Because it has answered a need of human nature, a need of making life harmonious, a need for the 'beauty and order' Sir Kenneth Clark commended to the townspeople of Swindon. If art is less important to us than to Melanesian islanders, do not think I mean to say that more or less simple communities are all made up of Michelangelos to a man. The American anthropologist Franz Boas says that in primitive societies 'the enjoyment of beauty is quite the same as among ourselves: intense among the few, slight among the mass'.

But in primitive societies the man who makes art is not looked upon as an odd fish. Art with them is an acceptable part of life, like eating or making love, though some are greedier, some more amorous.

With us, it is not so much the artist who has changed in his fundamental nature. It is society—you and me. In our society, devoted to making money, we are naturally less inclined to engage in art ourselves, naturally less tolerant of someone else who makes useless things such as pictures and poems, someone else who cares more than we do for order and 'beauty'—if that word must be used. Eric Gill wanted a society in which order and beauty were important values. He wanted society to change. But is society going to change, is the artist going to be accepted—much more, is art going to become part of our natural order of things— just through exhibiting art that exists already, with guide lecturers, or programme notes, to explain it?

Bringing art to everyone, as the Arts Council are trying to do it, *may* do something towards making us, as an audience, as a passive audience, accept and enjoy art, and value it in human life.

It may. . . . But as long as we go on talking in our reports of working for 'the future of the arts', go on thinking of art as something isolated, as *a thing by itself*, as long as we go on putting so much of the emphasis on exhibiting the ready-made, then we risk fossilizing art. We may even encourage a rigid preference for art of the past, already classified and evaluated. We may encourage a miserable contempt for the new, and end up by establishing one fossil instead of another, establishing the active dictatorship of a democratic academy instead of the would-be dictatorship of the old aristocratic academy. In short, organizing art for people to go and see, and hear, may wreak damage, *unless* we can couple it directly with two things: helping each of us— the professional included—to develop whatever capacity for art we have; and helping all of us to think deeply, feel deeply, why we are human; why we were born; and what this queer life of individuals in communion with each other implies.

Myself, I think that involves feeling deeply the 'numinous'— the sense of holiness. Not religion in the orthodox, organized sense; that I do not mean (though, incidentally, anthropologists have shown us that in some primitive societies art and religion are quite separate). I mean especially the free, undogmatic sense of the holiness of the most generous of possible relationships between men; between the nations of men, as well. Let the Arts Council go on with their exhibitions, concerts, and plays. But on top of that I want to see them increase enormously their encouragement to everyone to develop what art may be in him (by which I do not mean that everyone should just be an amateur actor in Eugene O'Neill's plays, or an amateur violinist inter- preting Bach). I want to see the Arts Council permeating all their activities, permeating all their officers, all their lecturers with a much bolder, more numinous sense of life and art, talking less of the 'future of art', and more of the health and future of society—if we could agree upon the definition of social health.

It is a fair analogy that we could never become able, well- exercised footballers by sitting on our behinds in the stand all the time and watching professionals play, or by looking at films of matches played thirty years ago. We should never appreciate the best points of professional football if we never had kicked a ball ourselves.

Pacific Service, 1946

20

ENGLISH NOVELS

I AM NOT giving this talk as a professional critic of novels, even less as a novelist. I have never written a novel, and I do not think I ever shall. For one thing, writing a novel is far too difficult, although we might not think so from the huge number which come out every year. Fiction is the most complicated of all kinds of art. Here is the writer, the one man or woman; outside him is the whole universe of the way in which you and I and everyone else behave. We are the limitless material. The novelist has to be very curious about us, and about himself, and even about ideas he may extract from our behaviour. His novel must begin, develop, and come to an end. All the senses of the novelist must be sharp, or at least the senses in which he is most perfect. If he has a theme, it cannot be put down baldly; or he would not be a novelist. The theme can only form itself from the way in which people talk, even more from the way in which they act. Turgenieff, for example, said that a novel began for him with a vision of people who solicited him by what they were and for whom he had to discover the right relationship.

The novel, then, is an extract of ourselves, our variety, our disorder, our untidiness; and it must itself be tidied into some degree of order. A great mess, a great human mess, has to be known; out of that accurate knowledge has to be shaped what we call a work of art, in such a way that we who read it are carried along, intrigued, delighted, impressed, convinced, and, if possible, satisfied.

As a reader of novels, I want to be satisfied as much as possible that the book I have just read gives me news about human life which I did not have before and which I am convinced is genuine. How much do I get that satisfaction and conviction from what we call the classical English novels, or the novels in the English tradition?

Before I attempt an answer, which means attempting to define the English tradition, I have to say that I may want other satisfactions—of design and shape, of style and language, but these are all subordinate: the more satisfying the novel is in these respects, the more certain should be its total power to satisfy me in its news about myself and all the other selves which make up humanity. There are no works of art, except small, unambitious ones, which are perfect. Henry James complained about Tolstoy's *War and Peace* that it was a great bag of a novel. It was disorderly, it was a 'large, loose, baggy monster'. There was life in it. But he preferred life rendered with economy and form. Henry James's own novels, after the baggy monster of *War and Peace*, often strike readers as having too much economy and form; which is to say that neither *War and Peace* nor *The Spoils of Poynton* by James is perfect. And I am pointing to this perfection and imperfection because it appears to me that the English novel is primarily marked by some, or at least by one, very striking imperfection; which, nevertheless, does not deprive the tradition of value—in fact, it is the tradition—and does not make some of the most eminent novels which conform so unsatisfying that there is no need to bother with them.

From Defoe to Dickens and after Dickens, and even to a point still, the English novel has been written by middle-class writers for a middle-class public. The middle class genuinely lives by an average of the social virtues. It is protector of those virtues. It is very much occupied—or it used to be—with asking whether the conduct of its members is right or wrong, virtuous or raffish. This has much affected both the scope and the depth of English fiction. Take first the readers of the novel. Forty-one years ago H. G. Wells published *Ann Veronica*. St. Loe Strachey (he was then editing the *Spectator*) led a delegation to the Home Secretary hoping that he could be enlisted to ban a novel so subversive of family life; not life, but family life, or the moral conduct of the middle classes. In 1895 Thomas Hardy had published a more remarkable novel, *Jude the Obscure*, in which, he said, 'the grimy features of the story go to show the contrast between the ideal life a man wished to lead, and the squalid real life he was fated to lead'. The Bishop of Wakefield thereupon did two things: he wrote a public letter to the press to say that he had thrown *Jude* into the fire (it was in the summer and Hardy rather doubted whether there would have been a fire in the palace), he wrote a private letter to the head of W. H. Smith's, of which the result was: 'the quiet withdrawal of the book from the library, and an assurance that any other books by the same author would be carefully examined before they were allowed to be circulated'.

Two of Hardy's comments were that he felt sure *Jude* 'makes for morality' and 'one cannot choose one's readers'. This fuss by readers over *Ann Veronica* and *Jude* is not so unimportant as it seems. The novelist cannot choose his readers and he cannot choose to be altogether separate from the society of which he and the readers are part. It is not a matter of choice. So from the beginnings of the English middle-class novel there have been restrictions, in which the novelist has acquiesced often without thinking about it, on what the novel shall be concerned with, how it shall be written, how far it shall go in the honest deduction from a set of observed characters in a situation.

In *Moll Flanders*, by Defoe, a prostitute tells how she lived. I do not think it would be fair to say that Defoe applies a wash of morality to her adventures. The morality was part of him, but living in the eighteenth century, at the beginning of the middle-class era, he could write much more plainly than Dickens, a hundred years later, could write about Nancy in *Oliver Twist*, who followed the same calling. Later again than Dickens, there was never a stronger advocate of duty than George Eliot, warm, sympathetic, tender, brilliant in the exploration of moral anxieties, yet careful—no, incapable—of going, as we say, too far; of going, we ought to say, far enough.

Writing perceptively of George Eliot, Henry James picked out the short, characteristic remark she made in her diary about reading one of the great novels of the world's literature, by Balzac, a writer whose ruthless curiosity does take him too far or far enough: 'We have just finished reading aloud *Père Goriot*, a hateful book'; and James adds the comment that for George Eliot the novel was not primarily a picture of life, 'but a moralized fable, the last word of a philosophy endeavouring to teach by example'. And do you remember, in *Adam Bede*, how outrageously George Eliot treated and neglected the poor eighteen-year-old Hetty, who had been weak enough and sinner enough to have an illegitimate child, and to kill the child, or expose it? Do you remember how she pushes her out of the novel once she is saved from the hangman? 'Poor wandering Hetty', she writes earlier, 'with the rounded childish face, and the hard unloving despairing soul looking out of it—with the narrow heart and narrow thoughts, no room in them'—she was soon going to have her child—'for any sorrows but her own, and tasting that sorrow with the more intense bitterness! My heart bleeds for her....' But there are limits to the quality if not the quantity of sympathetic blood which will come from the moral heart of George Eliot.

The English novel, then, is apt only to go so far, it is apt to avoid or to twist the logic of events, it is apt to assume that the best can be reached without a steady gaze at the worst. Perhaps I can illustrate this rather hard saying if I repeat two remarks made to me lately by a living novelist. We were talking about a new book of translations by the Russian storyteller Leskov, who never avoided the logic of a character or a situation. The novelist said he wished English fiction had not been so weak in portraits of clergymen, in which Leskov happens to excel.

Do not reply at once, 'haven't you read *The Warden* by Trollope?'—because, on the whole, it is true that our novelists have been shy of the deeper portraiture of clergymen. And why? Being the vessel and protector of the morality of the middle class, the clergyman cannot be analysed as a human being, weak as all the rest of us are weak. His second remark was that it would have been much healthier for English fiction if we, too, in the eighteenth century, had been given one of those vast autobiographies, like the confessional autobiography of Rousseau or Restif de la Bretonne, which attempt to tell all or most of the truth.

It is true that we, as readers, have changed and that the novel has changed (though not entirely) after blows with sandbags, such as Hardy's *Jude the Obscure* or *Ulysses* by Joyce (and that in spite of dying complaints by Tennyson of how novelists and others were feeding the budding rose of boyhood with the drainage of their sewer; Tennyson's attitude is one which some of us still, in good moralistic faith, maintain). Yet the preoccupation with guilt and moral anguish often continues—for instance in the novels of Mr. Graham Greene; but a particular we may notice is that Mr. Greene is at one with his own sinners. He assumes that both we and he are fallible, whereas Dickens and

George Eliot at times appear to address the morally infallible reader as morally infallible authors. Not you, dear family reader, not I, would behave as these bad people I present to you behaved.

You may call the English tradition of the novel Protestant (even as it continues in Graham Greene, who is a Catholic), Puritan, moral, or middle-class. Whatever it is, I should once have inclined to condemn it as a tradition which lacked intellectual integrity, in contrast to the much older tradition of English poetry, to argue that it was a tradition of novelists who were not honest enough and not artists enough. But I have not the pride or the insolence now to be quite so sure of that, or at any rate to fling the stone of condemnation. We should have the honesty and the strength in our day to see where the traditional imperfections lie—or the traditional twist—and we have really been given too much of that kind of criticism I have heard described lately as 'putting wreaths around well-loved names'. Yet if our novelists have been morally occupied, and if that made them, and damaged them, if that has led to concealments and evasions, and a partial view of life, if it has prevented them from using as fully as they might have done admirable powers of the heart and the head, an admirable ability to see, to feel, to imagine, to contrive (in which Dickens, for example, is among the masters of the world), we have to remember one thing. Our novelists belong to us. They have been dealing with us, with a people who were, or were more than we are still, morally occupied and morally anguished. If that is where our lives have been tense, it is where also our fiction must have found its own tensity, and its most genuine interest.

I wish English fiction had gone further, could have gone further, as far, say, into life as Balzac's novels or as the novels of the great Russian masters of the nineteenth century. But that is rather to wish that our own nature had been different. Even outside the limits of their art, outside their own intentions, outside as much news of life as they give without consideration of time, place, and nationality, one compelling reason for reading the masters of English fiction is: they tell us, even by what they do not tell, so very much of our own English moral constitution and moral limitations; a self-knowledge of the healthiest kind.

Home Service, 1949

21

'MOONFLEET' AND JOHN MEADE FALKNER

'I ONCE found him at lunch', wrote one of John Meade Falkner's friends, 'just finishing the *Odyssey* in the original for the fifteenth time.' That is a clue helping to explain why *Moonfleet* is one of the exciting adventure stories of our literature. If I think through such stories—most of them are far better known —I am convinced that few are so well written, have quite so peculiar a distinction, or present a better narrative. You may object 'Then why isn't *Moonfleet* better known?' And I am not sure that I can reply adequately or say why so very few readers seem to be aware of *Moonfleet*; why, in fact, so precise and distinguished a book (it is in the class of Stevenson's *Kidnapped* or *Treasure Island*) has not acquired the authority and celebrity of a minor classic.

Partly the answer may be in the peculiar life and character of the author. He died in 1932, a Wiltshire man, born in the Vale of Pewsey at Manningford Bruce, and brought up for the most part in Dorset near the scenes described in *Moonfleet*. His father was a parson first in Dorchester, next at Weymouth. Nothing peculiar so far. But he was not a professional author. He was a business man; and the fundamental peculiarity is that Falkner lived two lives, the life of a scholar and the life of an armament manufacturer—since he was chairman of the armament firm of Armstrong-Whitworth.

It was by accident that his professional life was of this kind and that he spent much of his time travelling around the world negotiating diplomatically and successfully with foreign governments. It happened this way. When he came down from Oxford (he had been a schoolboy at Dorchester Grammar School, then at Marlborough) he entered the family of the vice-chairman of Armstrong's as tutor to his children. He was trusted, liked, and indispensable; and was given a post in the firm, becoming chairman during the First World War.

Falkner was an able business man; but it would be hard to imagine anyone less like an industrial chieftain, in behaviour or in looks. An old Wiltshire friend of his described him for me. Very tall—about six foot six in his socks—very thin, with a stoop (his friends knew him as 'Long John'), and with lively eyes in a long narrow head. He was born out of the time of aeroplanes, twelve-inch guns, and penny newspapers. He used to say that he had 'a mediaeval mind'. And these two friends, Falkner and this Wiltshire girl, used to go round visiting churches—his long, thin six-foot-six curved grotesquely over a bicycle. His friend Thomas Hardy described himself as 'churchy'. Falkner was 'churchy' in the same and an extra sense; he was a devout Christian, unlike Hardy, and also a man who knew, understood, and was in love with the past. And since in any village the past is most immediately present in the church, Falkner never looked at a new place without entering the church first of all. He hated modernity. He would not have modern furniture in his house in the cathedral close at Durham—even in his servants' rooms. He hated having his photograph taken (if he was photographed in a group he would turn his face away). But mediaeval mind or no, he was full of life—a brilliant, unexpected, enthusiastic, perverse talker, a man of the world, not pompous, but always ready to tell jokes against himself.

His scholarship was deep and curious; he knew much of Byzantine archaeology, heraldry, mysticism, neo-Platonism, demonology, church architecture, church music, illuminated manuscripts. He knew the libraries of Europe—especially the Vatican Library. The Pope gave him a gold medal he reserved for scholars. When he died, Falkner left the Pope £500 for the Vatican Library, in memory of the happiness of working there. He wrote—I suppose wrote his novels—in a clear handwriting, based on mediaeval manuscripts; and living at Durham, he became Librarian of the Cathedral with its rich mediaeval possessions. There a friend of mine, fresh from Germany, a scholar of cathedral architecture, was introduced to him in the dark house. 'How extraordinary,' he thought, seeing the missals, the furniture, the paintings, drinking the port and savouring all the evidences of great wealth, 'that in England even cathedral librarians can live in this manner.' He was absent-minded; so I gather from a story the late Lady Oxford told of him. At the time of the split between Asquith and Lloyd George, he took the chair at a Liberal meeting up north, entertaining Asquith and his wife during their visit. He took them for a walk; suddenly, after they had gone a longish way, they realized Falkner had no boots on. He was striding along, his six-foot-six in bed-room slippers.

That was the man who wrote *Moonfleet*. A man, another of his old friends told me, it was wonderful to meet and know, especially when you were young; a man who exercised the most extraordinary fascination, to whom many people now living owe much of their spiritual and intellectual development. And in the man—the peculiarity of him—is part of the reason why *Moonfleet* is not a familiar title like *Kidnapped* or *Westward Ho!* In a world of imperfect readers, justified fame does not always come to a good writer unless he blows his own trumpet; or allows others to blow it for him. One did not have the indecency to advertise in the Middle Ages; and in Falkner's mediaeval mind there was no room for self-advertisement. He did not need to push himself as an author; and he did not want to push himself. He was glad that some people thought well of his novels. That was enough. His books were a by-product of a full, completed life. So, as we read by fashion, Falkner's books to-day (though he has his small circle of devotees) are not very much read.

There are three of them—I am talking only of novels, though among other things he wrote are two of Murray's Guides, those old and best of all guides to English counties, a book on Bath, some poems, and at least one short story. *Moonfleet* was the second of his novels, published in 1898. The first was *The Lost Stradivarius*, the last (what good titles they all have) was *The Nebuly Coat*. *The Lost Stradivarius* concerns a man who finds a lost violin in his rooms at Oxford, and whose face is turned white by seeing the vision of ultimate evil. *The Nebuly Coat*, a more complicated story, wonderfully re-creates the feel of a decayed Dorset church, a story of murder and the misfortunes of a noble house, poking some good incidental fun at the mock-mediaevalism in architecture of Sir Gilbert Scott. Curious, entertaining novels, suggesting more than they say, full of Falkner's out-of-the-way scholarship. But they have not the swiftness, the economy, the vividness, the sheer story-telling virtuosity of *Moonfleet*. When I read it, it was like reading a story again as a child. There was nothing to do but surrender and continue. Smuggling stories usually have a certain cheapness and falsity, a sham old-world quality. *Moonfleet* is actual. I envy anybody reading it for the first time—being with the boy in the dark, in the smuggling hiding-place under the church; climbing up the vast white cliff with a broken leg, by a sheep-path, to escape the preventive men; lying on a bed of bracken in the old underground Purbeck quarry, the cave that opens onto the sea. The title of the book tells you —if you know Dorset—exactly where most of it takes place: the church is the now fragmentary church of Fleet, overwhelmed in a storm in 1824, when the sea broke through the Chesil Bank; and there are still brasses in the church to the family of Mohun— *Moonfleet*.

I think this is so much the best of Falkner's books because he plays it out in the landscape which meant most to him in his life—the Dorsetshire landscape, with all its human association, which he had absorbed with absolute clarity into his conscious-ness as a boy. So, more than *The Nebuly Coat* and *The Lost Stradivarius* with their very agreeable load of scholarship, it was an act of his being; actually part of himself. The Dorset coast, with the Chesil Bank, the cliffs, and the quarry workings, was to Falkner precisely what the Scotland of *Kidnapped* was to Steven-son. There Falkner could not go wrong, he could not slow up such a personal, Dorset story with the odd rewards of his scholarship.

One of Falkner's critics, Mr. Pritchett, has complained— rightly, too—that his novels would be better if he had been more interested in the human beings he peopled them with. He had not the novelist's interest in the interactions of human behaviour; but that is of less account in such an adventure story; what mattered in *Moonfleet* was to give it a shape, to give it richness, to know what to leave out, to keep the story on the move. More-over, *Moonfleet* is a book with a consistent, personal tone. Like Falkner himself, it works a fascination, it works a spell, basically because the writing itself is personal and exquisite, just enough to call out the scene and the action, not enough to obtrude and become irritating. That is so from page one to the last surprising scene of the wreck on the Chesil Bank. The style is slightly remote, slightly 'period', getting the time of the story, yet always real; and sometimes Falkner will invent or borrow just the right word. When the lease of the Mohune Arms, at Moonfleet, is signed and sealed, Falkner writes of the wax falling on the parchment: then, he says, there was 'a swealing of the parchment under the hot wax'. A 'swealing'. A dialect word, I believe; and how neatly it describes the slight noisy crinkling of parchment under sealing-wax, how it drives in a dramatic incident, how it shows Falkner's sensitive regard of detail!

It may explain how curiously and convincingly Falkner goes to work, how he mixes action, knowledge, and sense of the Great Good Place, if I quote from the chapter called The Escape'. Elzevir and the boy have escaped from the preventive men, he has carried the boy up the cliff and reached the mouth of their hiding-place in the land of the old marble quarries:

'Although I knew little of these quarries, and certainly was in evil plight to take note of anything at that time, yet afterwards I learnt much about them. Out of such excavations comes that black Purbeck Marble which you see in old churches in our country, and I am told in other parts of England as well. And the way of making a marble quarry is to sink a tunnel, slanting very steeply down into the earth, like a well turned askew, till you reach fifty, seventy, or perhaps one hundred feet deep. Then from the bottom of this shaft there spread out narrow passages or tunnels, mostly six feet high, but sometimes only three or four, and in these the marble is dug. These quarries were made by men centuries ago, some say by the Romans themselves; and though some are still worked in other parts of Purbeck, those at the back of Anvil Point have been disused beyond the memory of man.

'We had left the stony tillage fields, and the face of the country was covered once more with the closest sward, which was just putting on the brighter green of spring. This turf was not smooth, but hummocky, for under it lay heaps of worthless stone and marble drawn out of the quarries ages ago, which the green vestment had covered for the most part, though it left sometimes a little patch of broken rubble peering out at the top of a mound. There were many tumble-down walls and low gables left of the cottages of the old quarrymen; grass-covered ridges marked out the little garden-folds, and here and there still stood a forlorn gooseberry-bush, or a stunted plum- or apple-tree with its branches all swept eastward by the up-Channel gales. As for the quarry shafts themselves, they too were covered round the tips with the green turf, and down them led a narrow flight of steep-cut steps, with a slide of soap-stone at the side, on which the marble blocks were once hauled up by wooden winches. Down these steps no feet ever walked now, for not only were suffocating gases said to beset the bottom of the shafts, but men would have it that in the narrow passages below lurked evil spirits and demons. One who ought to know about such things, told me that when St. Aldhelm first came to Purbeck, he bound the old Pagan gods under a ban deep in these passages, but that the worst of all the crew was a certain demon called the *Mandrive*, who watched over the best of the black marble. And that was why such marble might only be used in churches or for graves, for if it were not for this holy purpose, the *Mandrive* would have power to strangle the man that hewed it.

'It was by the side of one of these old shafts that Elzevir laid me down at last. The light was very low, showing all the little unevennesses of the turf: and the sward crept over the edges of the hole, and every crack and crevice in steps and slide was green with ferns. The green ferns shrouded the walls of the hole, and ruddy brown brambles overgrew the steps, till all was lost in the gloom that hung at the bottom of the pit.

'Elzevir drew a deep breath or two of the cool evening air, like a man who has come through a difficult trial.

'"There," he said, "this is 'Joseph's Pit', and here we must lie hid until thy foot is sound again. Once get to the bottom safe, and we can laugh at Posse, and hue-and-cry, and at the King's Crown itself."'

That is composed and careful writing of a fine order. The prose of a novelist who is a poet as well. As a poet (his poems, or a selection of them, have been privately printed), Falkner with his concern for the past and his eye for the immediate belongs to the school of his friends Hardy and Kipling. I do not say he wrote illuminating poetry, but his best poems are skilful, neat, and touching—and to touch was Thomas Hardy's aim. He varies from the ballad, such as the smuggling ballad that prefaces *Moonfleet*:

> But the bold Preventive man
> Primes the powder in his pan
>   And cries to the Posse, Follow me.
> We will take this smuggling gang,
> And those that fight shall hang
>   Dingle dangle from the execution tree,
>   Says the Gauger:
>   Dingle dangle with the weary moon to see—

to poems, such as 'After Trinity', showing an attraction of sentiment, of form, and nicety of words which is also part of the attraction of *Moonfleet* and his other novels. Part of it goes:

> *Post pugnam pausa fiet;*
>   Lord, we have made our choice;
> In the stillness of autumn quiet,
>   We have heard the still, small voice.
> We have sung *Oh where shall wisdom?*
>   Thick paper, folio, Boyce.
>
> Let it not all be sadness,
>   Not *omnia vanitas*,
> Stir up a little gladness
>   To lighten the *Tibi cras*;
> Send us that little summer
>   That comes with Martinmas,
>
> When the still cloudlet dapples
>   The windless cobalt-blue,
> And the scent of gathered apples
>   Fills all the store-rooms through,
> The gossamer silvers the bramble,
>   The lawns are gemmed with dew.
>
> An end of tombstone Latinity,
>   Stir up sober mirth,
> Twenty-fifth after Trinity,
>   Kneel with the listening earth:
> Behind the Advent trumpets
>   They are singing Emmanuel's birth.

This sincere writer who delighted to enrich Burford Church in Oxfordshire with crosses, altar frontals, crucifix, and candlesticks which he had acquired on his armament journeys around Europe, was buried at his own wish under Burford Church tower, beneath the place of the pre-Reformation rood. He was a pre-Reformation character who lived intensely enough in his chosen worlds of the past to be alive in them and in his own world, and to make his words quick and not dead.

Get *Moonfleet*. Get his other books if you can. Get his limpid short story of a Byzantine princess called *Charalampia*, which was published in the *Cornhill* in 1916.[1] The only thing, alas, you can never get hold of will be the fourth novel he wrote, which was 'snatched by a thief who mistook the case in which it was contained for a cash case, on the Newcastle Station platform'. It was Falkner's only copy of the manuscript, and he never recovered it.

[1] And republished, with some of Falkner's poems, in the second number of *The Mint A Miscellany of Literature, Art and Criticism*, in 1948.

West of England, 1945

22

COBBETT IN WILTSHIRE

WILLIAM COBBETT was a busybody, a politician, a political journalist, and a farmer, plain but by no means simple, insufferably determined, immensely opinionated, frequently wrong in his opinion, unquenchably curious, firm in his belief that large cities were mainly inhabited by drones, and that the primary welfare of England depended upon the land and those who worked the land. After all, farming is still, even in 1949, the largest of all our industries, employing the most numerous single body of men; and farming in the eighteen-twenties, when Cobbett began his rural riding, was severely hit by a multiplicity of causes.

So this egoistic democrat, who was himself the child of a small Hampshire farmer, and who always remembered the days when he had worn a smock-frock and carried a wooden bottle, like a shepherd's boy on the Downs, rode round and round about, to see, if he could, the condition of the farms, the farmers, the farm workers, the parsons, and the landlords, in all the counties of England.

Things were wrong. Cobbett had his own somewhat peculiar ideas of why they were wrong. His energy and temperament compelled him to collect, or complete, the evidence for his ideas. So upon horseback, in all weathers, when he was over fifty, he began his celebrated rides. In the West, the county of which he recorded most was Wiltshire; and since I live there, I shall consider for the most part Cobbett's Wiltshire evidence.

Agriculture in the world is about ten thousand years old; and by no means so old as that in the British Isles; and when Cobbett rode up and down, agriculture was over the crest from its older and cruder phases into its modern shape. I live myself in a village in North Wiltshire, surrounded by cold and deep land which was a forest of oaks until well into historic times. A few descendants of those oak trees are scattered about in the fields. Clearances of the forest can hardly have begun until after the

Saxon invasions, so that agriculture in my parish is not even two thousand years old. The divisions of the land, the boundaries of the farms, the utilization of the soil, are still affected by the Saxon revolution in farming and by the feudal system into which it changed.

When Cobbett arrived, my own parish was only, in those very years, by an enclosure act, discarding the remnants of the old feudal system. The open fields worked in common by farmers whose houses, buildings, and yards were grouped together in the village, were at last split up and enclosed into individual farms. The water-logged land was not suitable for corn, and was dangerous for sheep in the winter months. Enclosure made it possible to drain the land and turn it into pasture for cattle and milk; and pasture it remains even now.

But just as some of the old oaks of the forest, the primaeval forest, or at least their descendants, remain in these pastures, so, in our village, our lives are still affected by remnants of feudalism. The open fields were enclosed—yes, but the landlord and the farmers could not be expected to pull down their houses and buildings and build new ones conveniently near the land apportioned to each new farm. So the old grouping of the farmsteads persists, inconveniently, to this day: four sets of houses, yards, and outhouses are grouped together within a hundred yards of each other.

The farming, then, which Cobbett investigated and described a hundred and twenty years ago, was rooted in conditions of a past which still was not dead, which still has not died in 1949, and which, in one sense, can never die. History studies the complex, the divided and subdivided roots of the present, and the roots are a living past. One thing merges into another, and one condition provokes another condition, *ad infinitum*. Thus when Cobbett entered Wiltshire in November 1821, when agriculture was deep in a transient depression which added itself to all the modifying historical influences upon the countryside, he remarked, as he was to remark so often in his rides, upon the miserable poverty of the farm workers he saw, not so far away from my village.

He was riding from Hurstbourn Tarrant in Hampshire to Marlborough. 'The labourers along here', he wrote, 'seem very poor indeed. Farm houses with twenty ricks round each, besides those standing in the fields; pieces of wheat, 50, 60 or 100 acres in a piece; but a group of women labourers . . . presented such an assemblage of rags as I never saw before even amongst the hoppers at Farnham, many of whom are common beggars. I never before saw *country* people, and reapers, too, looking so miserable in appearance as these. There were some very pretty girls, but ragged as colts and pale as ashes. The day was cold, too, and frost hardly off the ground; and their blue arms and lips would have made any heart ache but that of a seat-seller or a loan-jobber.'

Here, too, was a condition, one of poverty, which provoked a counter-condition. The steps could be traced between these miserable, ragged men and women and children, between their misery in a transient depression and all the legislative and social steps which have put shoes on the feet of the children, given them schools and school meals, given their fathers a living wage, and taken themselves and their mothers off the land.

I have twice spoken of a transient depression in agriculture at the time of Cobbett's *Rural Rides*. What was the depression? What was its nature and how was it caused? From the *Rural Rides* themselves, and from Cobbett's forcible but muddled views, his exclamations and his anger and his vituperation, it would not be so easy to give an answer. Cobbett's own reasoning is not much more reasonable than a farm-worker's song which was current in Wiltshire, and perhaps in Hampshire as well, around this time. The song declared that the farm-workers were 'pinched in their bellies and pinched in their clothes'.

> Here's first to those farmers who do sell the corn
> And they are all as big rogues as ever were born;
> They are never contented, but still they have none,
> If the land were to yield fifty bushels for one—

And then in five more stanzas it goes through a list of rogues who should all swing together on the gallows, the mean landlord, the thieving miller, the cheating butcher, and the cheating baker who mixes bean flour and alum into the loaves. Cobbett's list of rogues and reasons is a bit more sophisticated, but not—alto-gether—more convincing.

The drones. The drones who eat the corn and eat the taxes. The drones especially in the big cities, and especially in the Wen, as he always names it, of London. Cobbett's drones included politicians who sat for rotten boroughs such as Wootton Bassett, or Old Sarum, or Calne, or Westbury, place-holders and middlemen such as the Quaker dealers in corn, sinecurists, pensioners; and parsons, creatures, wrote Cobbett, when he got to Wylye, 'that have an inheritance in the public carcase, like the maggots that some people have in their skins'. The remark was prompted by a non-resident rector of Wylye, who had a living elsewhere in Hampshire. Cobbett hated these pluralist clergymen who used tithe, a tax upon the land, to breed families of corn-devouring idlers, when tithe, he maintained, had originally been granted to unmarried parsons for their living and for distribution among the poor, and not as a 'premium for breeding'. But the worst rogue of all to Cobbett was the new kind of landlord, industrialists and financiers turned squire—turned into merciless 'Squires of Change Alley', who had built up their big estates from the smaller holdings of the yeomen and the lesser gentry ruined by the changes in agriculture in the preceding fifty years.

What Cobbett did not see—or did not see clearly—was the complicated nature of these agricultural changes and the depression. The high prices which farm produce had commanded in the French wars had collapsed after 1815. Farmers had to retrench, and retrenched at the cost of labour. That was one cause. But the deeper cause was this revolution in agriculture. Enclosures in Wiltshire alone had transformed the rural economy in Cobbett's lifetime. Small farmers became farm-labourers, farm-labourers lost their rights in the waste land of the manors, on which they could pasture geese and a cow and get their firing. Industry was also being transformed and collected into the factories, so that the Wiltshire farm-workers' families no longer could eke out their living, for example, by spinning wool at home. The war raised the cost of living, and the post-war depression broke upon a countryside which had not had time to readjust itself to a new world.

Farming was changing from subsistence-farming to capitalized farming, to feed the new proletariat of the cities created by industrial capital. The farm worker who had boarded with the farmers and lived off the produce of the land which he worked, now had to live on his own and live (in a reign of high prices) on a wage. He had to buy—the writer of that song was right—for the first time from the butcher and the baker and the brewer. Yet these rogues of his imagination were not the causes of his distress, but parallel symptoms of that distress.

Cobbett was too much inclined to take symptoms for causes. The husband of 1949 looks at his dinner and says, 'Starch again.' The wife replies, 'Go and see the Food Minister.'

Cobbett, with the same near-sightedness of a contemporary, blamed (though they were not free of blame) his squires of Change Alley, the politicians, the parsons, the corn dealers, and so on. The canal at Devizes, he remarked, was 'the great channel through which the produce of the country is carried away to be devoured by the idlers, the thieves and the prostitutes who are all tax-eaters, in the Wens of Bath and London'. He maintained that the corn only went to his 'tax-eaters'. If Wiltshire corn was exchanged between two sets of workers, industrial and agricultural, if a waggon-load of wheat went off from the Vale of Pewsey in the morning, and came back in the evening loaded with the produce of industry, instead of coming back more or less empty, as it did, then the Wiltshire people might see it go without tears in their eyes.

Cobbett was too near events on his *Rural Rides*—and too bigoted —to note the complexity of their causes, so you must read his famous book cautiously. None the less, Cobbett's picture of the poverty, misery, and depopulation in Wiltshire and in Hampshire and elsewhere in the eighteen-twenties is in itself true, moving and brilliantly recorded. His book is one of those curious cases of literature outliving the polemic causes which brought it into being.

West of England, 1948

23

WORDSWORTH, NATURE, AND THE LAKES

You MAY RECALL a guilty passage in Byron's letters in which he turns upon romanticism.

He complains that poets of the day, including himself and Wordsworth, 'are all in the wrong . . . are upon a wrong revolutionary poetical system, or systems, not worth a damn in itself'. He had much else to say at one time and another—for example about 'two sorts of Naturals; the Lakers, who whine about nature because they live in Cumberland; and their under-sect (which someone has maliciously called the "Cockney School"), who are enthusiastical for the country because they live in London'. In the decay, in the new softness of English poetry, Byron thought that 'the best sign of amendment will be repentance and new and frequent editions of Pope and Dryden'. It is an opinion which has been repeated in different ways since by poets as diverse as Hopkins and Mr. Eliot and Mr. Auden. Hopkins found in Keats—Byron's 'tadpole of the Lakes'—an 'unmanly and enervating luxury': he found Dryden 'the most masculine of our poets', one whose 'style and rhythms lay the strongest stress of all our literature on the naked thew and sinew of the English language'.

The masculine poet, such as Dryden—or the masculine painter such as Poussin—deals, above all, in the actions of men; desert man too much for nature—particularly for nature as a benign force—and the masculinity is diluted too much by its opposite. Instead of the thew and resilient hardness of Dryden, one has what Coleridge called 'the mild and philosophic pathos of Wordsworth'; one has a poetry, in all its simplicity and gravity, which corresponds to the peculiar, palpable femininity of the Lake District—at least in its milder times and aspects. The Lake District is one of the chief clues to understanding the romantic 'revolution' in the arts; and it was not, as we are inclined to

138

believe, discovered by Wordsworth, however much it has been vulgarized and popularized as a consequence of Wordsworth's poetry and Wordsworth's residence among the mountains. The discovery was made long before Wordsworth was born, in the course of that great picturesque exploration of Great Britain through the eighteenth century. On the whole, it is true to say that the picturesque places, the 'beauty spots' which have filled the guide-books ever since, down to Murray and Ward Lock, were explored, celebrated, and established by painters. Painters tramped the lanes and the tracks; the poets, who saw the engravings after their pictures, came later. Celebrated as a Lakeland pioneer, the poet Thomas Gray did not reach the Lakes, with a landscape mirror in his pocket for picturing the finest scenes, until 1769. Lakeland etchings after William Bellers had been published in 1753, sixteen years earlier than Gray's visit, and seventeen years before Wordsworth was born.

The spirit in all this picturesque exploration was to find those scenes, reduced to a picture either by the pencil or on the pocket mirror (this landscape mirror is described carefully for tourists in the *Guide to the Lakes* by Thomas West), which afforded one sentimental pleasure—scenes which afforded one pleasure arising from the feelings rather than from reason. All was a matter of sentiment and taste, a matter of indulging all the sensations, through all the degrees of beauty to all the degrees of sublimity. A matter also of discovering—in Wales, in the Lakes, or in Scotland, at home and in nature—what the new taste of the century had already discovered in its favourite Old Masters.

Thus Thomas West, who published his famous guide when Wordsworth was an eight-year-old child at Cockermouth, arranged the Lakes in what he called 'an order more agreeable to the eye and grateful to the imagination'. 'The changes of scene', he continued, 'is from what is pleasing to what is surprising; from the delicate touches of *Claude*, verified on Coniston Lake, to the noble scenes of *Poussin*, exhibited on Windermere; and from these, to the stupendous, romantic ideas of *Salvator Rosa*, realized on Derwent-lake.'

This was the climate of mind in which Wordsworth grew up—the climate of the longing, yearning soul which was to be flattered by attention to the beauties of natural scenery. And nowhere were those instruments of flattery more concentrated than in the Lakes. Nowhere, as Wordsworth wrote in his own *Guide to the Lakes*, 'within so narrow compass, may be found an equal variety in the influences of light and shadow upon the sublime and beautiful features of the landscape'. I have said elsewhere that if you wish to understand the common, the commonplace romantic vision, stand in the porch of the Victorian hotel and look down on Buttermere. Watch mood diluting reality, watch the romantic soul diffused in the water-glowing air between lake and mountain and sky, embracing and modifying everything. Watch a few small bits of cloud, white below the black mountain level, wisping above the lake. Wordsworth, again in his *Guide*, said that such clouds were 'pregnant with imagination for the poet'. He wrote that 'vapours exhaling from the lakes and meadows after sunrise, in a hot season, or, in moist weather, brooding upon the heights, or descending towards the valleys with inaudible motion, give visionary character to everything around them'. Those silvery vapours are celebrated in *The Prelude*.

One may add to all this an extraordinary sweetness in the Lakes, in the taste of the air, in the light, in the conjunction of green fertility, reflecting water, and small mountain—that sweetness, that palpable femininity of which I spoke. Stern the Lakes are as well, with a sternness which appealed to the deliberate and the strong in Wordsworth; but it seems to me rather the tender aspect which is reflected in the structural substance of his verse.

Growing up, as I say, in such a climate of the mind, Wordsworth would have been certain to find the sweetness, the sublimities, and the visionary character of the Lake District, even if he had not been born on its western edge at Cockermouth, even if he had not been educated in among the Lakes at Hawkshead, with Windermere two miles away. As Byron wrote, Southey, Wordsworth, and Coleridge 'rambled over half Europe' and saw 'Nature in most of her varieties'. Wordsworth, like the topographical artists and the picturesque travellers, was a collector of scenery. But not—and here is the point—not finally and deeply for sentimental ends, not for flattering the soul, not for self-indulgence in the correspondence of feelings; not, as with the mere moralists who were a little disturbed by this romantic self-flattery, for what Wordsworth called in *The Prelude* 'Nature's secondary grace':

> The charm more superficial that attends
> Her works, as they present to Fancy's choice
> Apt illustrations of the moral world,
> Caught at a glance, or traced with curious pains.

The difference between Wordsworth — or Wordsworth and Coleridge—and the nature-tipsy poets and painters and aestheticians from whom, inevitably, they took so much, is that they were little and Wordsworth and Coleridge were unusually big, were lofty and speculative minds; they dignified something trivial into an instrument of relation and meaning.

The Prelude—particularly the less cautious *Prelude* of 1805-6—all the same exhibits Nature almost as God himself; not as a mirror for the emotions, not as a sentimental something; but as a Being, a source (localized, as it happens, inevitably among the Lakes) by which the emotions are educed, are trained, are given self-knowledge, dignity, and purpose. Nature, not caught at a glance, but entered into; training one into love which acts and exists only with Imagination. Imagination *The Prelude* defines as:

> . . . but another name for absolute power
> And clearest insight, amplitude of mind
> And Reason in her most exalted mood.

So in the Conclusion of *The Prelude*, 'This faculty'—this Imagination—'hath been the moving soul of our long labour':

> We have traced the stream
> From darkness and the very place of birth
> In its blind cavern, whence is faintly heard
> The sound of waters; follow'd it to light
> And open day, accompanied its course
> Among the ways of Nature, afterwards
> Lost sight of it bewilder'd and engulph'd,
> Then given it greeting, as it rose once more
> With strength, reflecting in its solemn breast
> The works of man and face of human life,
> And lastly, from its progress have we drawn
> The feeling of life endless, the great thought
> By which we live, Infinity and God.

The loftiness of the result—the result in *The Prelude*, above all in this concluding book—no one can question; but there is much in the process, in Wordsworth's view of nature, in his nearly admitted pantheism, which is questionable, and was indeed questioned, for example, by Coleridge; and also by Blake.

In discussing *The Prelude*, Herbert Read quoted Coleridge's suggestion to Wordsworth for the great philosophic poem to be called 'The Recluse'. Man was to be treated of in contact with *external* nature. The poet was to inform the senses from the mind, and not compound a mind out of the senses. *The Prelude* does pay some heed to that injunction. Wordsworth does include that passage on Imagination as 'Reason in her most exalted mood' and on the necessity of Imagination; but, all through, the active presence and personification of Nature—Nature with a capital—gets attended to more than mind, or reason, or imagination.

Coleridge had been bewitched himself by pantheism, had realized the bitterness of its root, and was clear that nature lives only in our life; clear, as he wrote in *Dejection*, that the passion and the life come from fountains inside us and cannot be won from outward forms. Admiration for his poems, reverence for his poems or no, he understood that Wordsworth was not so clear on the matter. Coleridge admitted 'that this inferred dependency of the human soul on accidents of birth-place and abode, together with the vague, misty, rather than mystic, confusion of God with the world, and the accompanying nature-worship, of which the asserted dependence forms a part, is the trait in Wordsworth's poetic works that I most dislike as unhealthy, and denounce as contagious'.

Blake was equally disturbed by Wordsworth's nature-worship; seeing in Wordsworth 'the natural man rising up against the spiritual man continually', and denying Wordsworth's statement that the powers needed for writing poetry are first observation and description, and second, sensibility. 'One Power alone makes a Poet,' Blake wrote against it, 'Imagination, the Divine Vision.'

And the nature-worshipping trait has been contagious. In his Life of Wordsworth Professor Harper confidently affirmed that no one could say 'Wordsworth's influence has had the effect of blunting the poetical sensibilities of our race'; which is precisely what Wordsworth's influence has done—partly through his deification of a benign nature, and his dependence upon it, partly through the loose and feminine structure of his verse and its approach to the simple speech, which naturally go with that deification, that degree of the desertion of man, at least for man represented only in his relations to nature. Like Constable in painting, Wordsworth in poetry begat a softness and a sentimentality, divorced from his cultivated insight, from which we still have not recovered. There it is: Byron's 'revolutionary system', the system 'not worth a damn'—the exaggeration was pardonable—which necessitated re-injections of Dryden and Pope.

Still, Blake and Coleridge both clearly apprehended the fault, both knew and said, again and again, that Wordsworth was a supreme poet. Hopkins acknowledged his greatness—above all (like Blake), in the *Intimations* ode. Human nature, he wrote, in a very few men sees something, receives a shock and 'is in a tremble ever since'. In Wordsworth when he wrote that ode, 'human nature got another of those shocks, and the tremble from it is spreading'. But Hopkins was severe on Wordsworth's manner of writing, on his weakness in the 'rhetoric' of literature by which he meant its 'common and teachable element'.

In one of his twelve observations on art, Poussin declared that the light of knowledge 'is never to be found whole or even in a large part in a single man': Perhaps, in our superstitious attitude to the arts, we do not acknowledge that—do not acknowledge the compound of dust inevitable in the clearest spirits. *The Prelude* is the major achievement of a major poet. Only one must read it with some *caveats* about Wordsworth's view of nature, his thought, and his style.

Third Programme, 1947

24

THE LOOK OF WORDSWORTH

THERE IS plenty of warrant for attempting to describe Wordsworth and his character apart from the poems which Wordsworth wrote, though the man and the poems do in fact agree—at least the man who was alive between 1797 and 1807, which are the years of his great poetry. Hazlitt has described him. De Quincey realized that we should not lose interest in Wordsworth. Using a Westmorland expression, he asked, '*What-like* was Wordsworth?' and gave his answer, which does not square altogether with Hazlitt's description. Herbert Read, a Yorkshireman writing about another man of Yorkshire descent, began his much criticized book on Wordsworth with a portrait, because he felt that 'to hold in our minds a clear image of the physical features of the man is a salutary preparation for the interpretation of his work and temperament'. I agree with the reason, though I do not altogether agree with the way in which Herbert Read picked over the visual evidence.

Wordsworth was twenty-eight in the year 1798, when the *Lyrical Ballads* were published; and thirty-seven when De Quincey met him at Grasmere after those moments of 'intense expectation' when he would have forgotten 'Charlemagne and all his peerage' if they had been behind him 'or Caesar and his equipage, or Death on his pale horse'. What-like then was Wordsworth in those years, more or less? What are we told by reminiscences and portraits? He was unimpressive until the face was turned upon you. 'His person', Dorothy Wordsworth had remarked, 'was not in his favour.' He was tallish, to be exact five foot ten. His shoulders were narrow and sloped quickly down. Hazlitt saw him first of all curiously dressed in a brown fustian jacket and striped pantaloons. His legs were unshapely, he walked in a lunging, rolling manner, and was neither slender nor graceful. But the face—how different from the round, illuminated lard which was the face of Coleridge! The colour was bronze. Brown hair straggled down over his forehead and past swollen, ugly ears to the shoulders. A great beak of a nose stuck out, seeming to occupy most of the length of his long countenance. The eyebrows were well marked, furrows came down from the nose around the mouth. Hazlitt noted these furrows of 'strong purpose and feeling' and 'a severe, worn pressure of thought about his temples'. But the two indices were the eyes and the mouth above a strong chin. It is curious how the descriptions of the eyes conflict. They were remarkable—everyone agrees to that. They were heavy-lidded, rather small than large under the arching of the eyebrows and the severity of the temples. According to Hazlitt they had a fire in them 'as if he saw something in objects more than the outward appearance'. According to De Quincey they were 'not under any circumstances bright, lustrous or piercing', unlike his sister's eyes which gleamed wildly and ardently. Their effect was at times 'fine, and suitable to his intellectual character'. 'After a long day's toil in walking,' says De Quincey, 'I have seen them assume an appearance the most solemn and spiritual that it is possible for the human eye to wear. The light which resides in them is at no time a superficial light; but, under favourable accidents, it is a light which seems to come from unfathomed depths: in fact, it is more truly entitled to be "the light that never was on land and sea", a light radiating from some far spiritual world, than any the most idealizing that ever yet a painter's hand created.' It may indeed have been a fierier light which came from the eyes in the great year of 1798 than in the more composed maturity of 1807. Leigh Hunt said they were eyes which would have suited Ezekiel or Isaiah—'half burning, half smouldering'. But who says a word about their colour?

The eyes, at any rate, speak for one element in Wordsworth's character and the character of his poetry, and the mouth for another element every bit as important. He was spiritual and he was sensual. Herbert Read makes much of this combination in his study of Wordsworth. He was spiritual, he was animal. But he goes too far and against the evidence when he reads a 'loose brutality' into the mouth. It was a wide mouth, with the lips firm and ample rather than full; sensual, yes, but also generous and tender. And while we are looking Wordsworth in the face, in the eyes, and in the mouth, we should recall at this point something else which Hazlitt recorded. The common notion is that Wordsworth had a face like a horse, and a cart-horse, strong, ugly, solemn, unrelieved. Hazlitt wrote there was also 'a convulsive inclination to laughter about the mouth, a good deal at variance with the solemn, stately expression of the rest of his face'. That has always seemed to me the clue about Wordsworth's appearance which most of us overlook; and I may mention that Wordsworth's physiognomy obviously repeats itself in more than one of his descendants who are alive now. I have observed in two of them exactly this contrast (they will excuse me for saying it) between solemnity, even heaviness, and a convulsive, hovering inclination to laughter; which is extraordinarily attractive. Dorothy Wordsworth, too, has described her brother's 'extremely thoughtful countenance', adding that 'when he speaks it is often lighted up by a smile which I think very pleasing'. To complete the picture, we must add the voice, from Hazlitt. It was a mixture of 'clear, gushing accents' with a 'deep guttural intonation, and a strong tincture of the northern burr, like the crust on wine'. Speech did not come from him torrentially. Dorothy Wordsworth remarked that 'you must be with him more than once before he will be perfectly easy in conversation'.

What we may conclude from this portraiture is that in his person (this might be said of living poets, for instance Mr. Auden or Mr. Eliot) Wordsworth was in many ways admirably 'unpoetical'. He was the inelegant Northerner controlling strong appetites in big or little. We know how frugally he and his sister could live with little money: for a strong appetite in little we have a description of him sitting down and 'attacking' a cheese. We know that he did not dislike alcohol, and that he took too much of it only once, in drinking a libation to the memory of Milton when he was an undergraduate. We know how immense passion swelled up in him when he was twenty-one or twenty-two and broke his incipient restraints and gave Annette Vallon a daughter, we know also how his power of self-control, if in the run of things it damaged him and led him into those conventional and harsh falsities which are so often condemned with too little point or charity, was also a power of almost unexampled self-culture. There were two or more Wordsworths in the 'gaunt and Don

Quixote-like' creature, intermixed and inseparable. Outwardly, that inelegant reserved Northerner, inwardly, the atomic heat. Outwardly, the countryman striding on awkward but efficient legs across the hills, the practical man who was able in growing cabbages and carrots or could take the mattock from Simon Lee and sever the tangled tree root, inwardly, the hypochondriac liable always to depression and melancholy, deliberate in his search for the roots of happiness. Wordsworth had plenty of personal warrant for writing retrospectively and prophetically:

> We poets in our youth begin in gladness
> But thereof comes in the end despondency and madness.

He described himself as of a 'stiff, moody, and violent temper' when a child. Coupled with that was the 'violence of affection' described in him as a young man by Dorothy Wordsworth—'a sort of violence of affection . . . which demonstrates itself every moment of the day, when the objects of his affection are present with him, in a thousand almost imperceptible attentions to their wishes, in a sort of restless watchfulness which I know not how to describe, a tenderness that never sleeps, and at the same time such a delicacy of manners as I have observed in few men'. Wordsworth's hypochondria is no doubt the explanation of those periods after his return from France which are blank in the record of his life. Coleridge wrote of his 'occasional fits of hypochondriacal uncomfortableness—from which, more or less, and at longer or shorter intervals, he has never been wholly free from his very childhood'; and he went on (the letter was written in 1804) 'he both deserves to be and is a happy man; and a happy man not from natural temperament, for therein lies his main obstacle . . . but . . . because he is a Philosopher, because he knows the intrinsic value of the different objects of human pursuit, and regulates his wishes in strict subordination to that knowledge'. That self-culture was one of the reasons which made the great, if then youthful, Coleridge feel himself 'a little man by his side', one of the reasons, too, for Coleridge's belief that a good poet was always a good man.

Herbert Read's *Wordsworth*, which so upset the circumspect scholars, is a book not to be overlooked if you are under the fascination of Wordsworth. It is one of the books which broke the platitudinous spell binding the study of the poems and the worship of the poet and made an end of evading the cavernous complexity of Wordsworth's character. I do not agree with it altogether, the evidence is sometimes misused, and Herbert Read assumes where the evidence is lacking or insufficient. The crux of the matter is this self-culture of Wordsworth and the hermetically cultivated sanity of his creative life. There is a passage I must quote. We know how Wordsworth changed from revolution into what we call reaction. Mr. Read gives as the cause Wordsworth's separation from Annette and the death of his passion for her during the nine years' interval of war with France. He writes: 'We grow to hate the object of a dead passion, but we do not acknowledge this to ourselves; we transfer that hatred to things associated with the dead passion. In this manner Wordsworth gradually renounced the cause of France and then the cause of revolution, and finally the cause of humanity.' There are several answers one could make—even that Annette and her brother were Royalists and against the Revolution when Wordsworth and she were in love, and when Wordsworth was a revolutionary; or that we do not know enough about Wordsworth and Annette to draw firm conclusions; or that Mr. Read forgets the parallel change in the sentiments of Coleridge, who had no French lover and daughter; or even that we have the example of the change of poetic hearts towards the Communist revolution, uncomplicated by Russian mistresses and daughters. But to press that analysis—here is the true answer—to press it, except perhaps as a contribution, is to deny the nature, value, and force of Wordsworth's cultivation of his own character, to remove the foundation, or so it appears to me, of a heroic greatness and of any clear ability to know 'the intrinsic value of the different objects of human pursuit'. This is the last thing which Mr. Read as a devotee of Wordsworth and Wordsworth's poetry wishes to do, or so I should think.

The essence of Wordsworth as a man is the combination of ordinary and extraordinary humanity and more than normally human power, of tough and of tender; which enabled him to look at the worst and the best, to realize the unity of man and to enter 'into the temple and the temple's heart'. One could get at him by sorting out the complementary differences between himself and Coleridge, even the physical differences between the long-nosed cart-horse and the fat gazelle; or in the record of their different ways of composition. Hazlitt tells us that Coleridge 'liked to compose in walking over uneven ground, or breaking through the struggling branches of a copse-wood; whereas Wordsworth always wrote (if he could) walking up and down a straight gravel-walk, or in some spot where the continuity of his verse met with no collateral interruption'. De Quincey confirms this by recording that Wordsworth liked to compose on the high-road. Or we have records of Coleridge being fascinated by the prison etchings of Piranesi, Wordsworth by Bewick's wood engravings in little, and by Rembrandt in great because Wordsworth could perceive in Rembrandt an analogy 'to his own mode of investing the minute details of nature with an atmosphere of sentiment'; also because Rembrandt could 'work something out of nothing', transforming 'the stump of a tree, a common figure, into an *ideal* object by the gorgeous light and shade thrown upon it'. Or contrast again the earnestness of Wordsworth and the bookishness of Southey. 'I have at all times endeavoured to look steadily at my subject', Wordsworth wrote, prefacing the *Lyrical Ballads*; and he complained in 1797 that Southey wrote '*too much at his ease*'—that he seldom

> 'feels his burthened breast
> Heaving beneath th' incumbent Deity.'

Wordsworth disliked Southey's 'finical' way of using books, Southey disliked having Wordsworth in his neat library. De Quincey described how Wordsworth 'tore his way into the heart' of a volume of Burke's collected writings with a knife which had been used for buttering toast. Coleridge's wonderful conversation flew down from the air, Wordsworth's was 'slow in its movement, solemn, majestic'. Coleridge read everything and scribbled a monologue of criticisms and comment around the margins, Wordsworth ate of fewer books and did not overflow into marginalia. Good qualities and great achievements exact their price, characters are mixed, and Wordsworth was neither deity nor saint. We have no more right to *complain* of Wordsworth's deficiencies than we have to complain of the great nose on his

sallow face.   The personal details I have given cannot be can-
celled.   They agree with the poems, they agree with:

> She sleeps in the calm earth, and peace is here.
> I well remember that those very plumes,
> These weeds, and the high spear-grass on that wall,
> By mist and silent rain-drops silvered o'er,
> As once I passed, did to my heart convey
> So still an image of tranquillity.
> So calm and still, and looked so beautiful
> Amid the uneasy thoughts which filled my mind,
> That what we feel of sorrow and despair
> From ruin and from change, and all the grief
> The passing shows of Being leave behind,
> Appeared an idle dream, that could not live
> Where meditation was.   I turned away
> And walked along my road in happiness.

Indeed such poetry can only come from those poets who are at
once tender and tough.

Third Programme, 1948

25

THE RHYTHMS OF POETRY

MOST ENGLISH POETS will remember being visited some years ago by the Librarian of the Lockwood Memorial Library at the University of Buffalo. He asked them all for manuscript drafts which would show how they had worked at a poem from conception to finality. After ten years the library has built up, so to say, a poetic workshop. In the library now there are 10,000 printed books of twentieth-century verse; there are 350 files of magazines from the 'Little Review' and, for example, 'New Verse' which I edited before the war, to the latest born 'little magazine'; and there are 3000 sets of these drafts or 'work sheets', some of which, according to the librarian, 'record with remarkable thoroughness the complete history' of the making of a poem. Next, the librarian asked a scholar, a psychologist, and two poets, one of them W. H. Auden, to explore and assess all this workshop material. Their findings were then published in a book you may have seen called *Poets at Work*. One of the contributors mentions the last poem in *The Shropshire Lad*, the one beginning 'I hoed and trenched and weeded,' because Housman in *The Name and Nature of Poetry* had described the way in which it was born. Two stanzas out of four had come to him complete and without difficulty as he was walking across Hampstead Heath from the Spaniards to the footpath to Temple Fortune. He wrote a third stanza during tea-time. The fourth stanza took Housman a year to perfect, passing through thirteen versions. So this poetic workshop or laboratory is meant rather to satisfy our curiosity over what the psychologist calls in the book 'the study of the creative process' in the individual. Its aim is not so much to help us to appreciate and enjoy the result of the process, which is the poem.

All this, I suppose, was bound to happen. It is a remarkable, stimulating, alarming enterprise; alarming because if you look at it in one way, it partakes of that nauseating concern-for-poetry by which we have come to evade the reading of poems for what they are; alarming, and yet no one was much alarmed except Mr. Auden, who wrote that 'the most significant fact about the Buffalo collection of manuscripts is that it exists, because one cannot imagine the idea occurring to anyone before the twentieth century. Until recently,' he went on, 'the concern of critics and public alike was a reader's concern with the final published product.' So Mr. Auden shied off the manuscripts and supplied instead some aphoristic observations about the poetic calling.

Of course an *ars poetica* and a psychology of poetry are not the same thing. I would suggest that the Buffalo workshop needs the complement of a workshop for unravelling the historical, as well as the personal, genesis of poetry. We need to know about the fundamental and more or less universal elements which twine together into that complexity of ordered language we call a poem. This *ars poetica* is the art of contriving rhythmical constructions out of language; and it is that element of rhythm which concerns me now. I shall start from two of those observations on the poetic calling which Mr. Auden contributed to *Poets at Work*.

'A poet' (I am quoting Mr. Auden) 'is before anything else, a person who is passionately in love with language. . . . "Why do you want to write poetry?" If the young man answers "I have important things I want to say", then he is not a poet. If he answers "I like hanging around words listening to what they say", then maybe he is going to be a poet.' This seems to me part of the fact, but not the whole of it. A poet, I should say, is before anything else a person who is passionately in love with language and exceptionally responsive to rhythm. So he is gifted to compel language into a special rhythmical order. Indeed, Mr. Auden goes on that 'Rhymes, metres, stanza-forms, etc., are like servants. If the master is just enough to win their affection and firm enough to command their respect, the result is an orderly, happy household. If he is too tyrannical, they give notice; if he lacks authority, they become slovenly, impertinent, drunken, and dishonest. The poet who writes "free verse" is the Robinson Crusoe on his desert island: he must do all his cooking, laundry, darning, etc., for himself. In a few exceptional cases this manly independence produces something original and impressive, but as a rule the result is squalor, empty bottles on the unswept floor and dirty sheets on the unmade bed.' Precisely: the opposite of free is controlled, and the foundation of this control, in this art of poetry, is rhythm.

Not, you will agree, a very new observation, but I doubt if at the present day we attend enough to this elemental necessity of rhythm. Aristotle tells us at once in the *Poetics* that poetry arises from our natural response to imitation and to harmony and rhythm; to which metres, he says, obviously belong. Yeats called a poem 'an elaboration of the rhythms of common speech and their association with profound feeling'. Mr. Eliot remembers how a poem or part of a poem 'may tend to realize itself first as a particular rhythm before it reaches expression in words'. Marxist critics such as Christopher Caudwell or Professor George Thomson agree to this obvious yet not always regarded fact that the language of poetry is rhythmical. Christopher Caudwell, taking one by one the characteristics of poetry, begins that 'poetry is rhythmic', has a 'marked rhythm, superimposed upon the "natural" rhythm of any language.'

But who was it who began to write about *poetry-for-the-eye*? About the effect of printing upon poetry? About modern poetry to be received only in silence through the eye as it runs across the lines, and not through the ear? If the printing of poems, indeed the writing of poems, a written literature instead of an oral literature, tends to flatten and loosen and weaken the rhythms of poetry (I am not sure that it does), mightn't we think this a decay? And yet, for example, Mr. Julian Symons, broadcasting a few weeks ago, maintained that the appeal of poetry by ear was a thing over and done with because of the changed basis of our society, and that the poetry of our time appeals to the verbal and visual sense of the individual reader. So we do not all agree about the primacy of a marked rhythm. Much accepted poetry of our time is indeed unrhythmical or only faint in its rhythms. Much poetry which is strongly rhythmical is read—and read sometimes on the B.B.C.—as though it was not rhythmical. That has been so for many years. Do you remember that broadcast which W. B. Yeats gave on modern poetry in 1936? 'When I have read you a poem,' he ended, 'I have tried to read it rhythmically; I may be a bad reader, or read badly because I am out of sorts, or self-conscious; but there is no other method. . . . To read a poem like prose, that hearers unaccustomed to poetry may find it easy to understand, is to form it into bad florid prose. If anybody reads or recites poetry as if it were prose from some public platform, I ask you, speaking for poets, living, dead or unborn, to protest in whatever way occurs to your perhaps youthful minds; if they recite or read by wireless, I ask you to express your indignation by letter.'

Very well: I can be excused for thinking and talking about poetry as an art of contriving rhythmical constructions out of language, when rhythm is being held as less important than the verbal shock or the unexpected metaphor or image. I can be excused for going back to the simplest rhythmical origins of poetry, and then coming forward again to show the rhythm remaining, but the simplicity becoming complexity.

The anthropological evidence. The music of verse is its total sound, the sound of the particular words in combination: rhythm is the sequence of pitch and time within that sound. Any one of us can affirm from our own daily experience that Aristotle was right in saying that rhythm is natural to us. Franz Boas the anthropologist declared that because rhythm, through whatever physiological reason, affected us emotionally, it therefore comes into all activities which have anything to do with our emotional life. Rhythm, he said, excites primitive men in religious songs and dances, compels them in war songs, and soothes them in melodies. Rhythm may tie us together, but in origin it is personal to each of us, physiologically: it does not begin in the things we do together, religiously or socially, but it prompts those religious and social activities, and it is prompted by them. Primitive peoples do not have poetry without music or without music and dancing. The lyrical or dithyrambic words may be very simple indeed, and scarcely, as we would say, a poem at all without music and without dance, without the stronger super-added sequences of rhythm.

The trouble about studying primitive poetry is that poetry is untranslatable, that primitive poetry is in languages we do not know and that we have to take it on trust from anthropologists. What appears to happen in the genesis of this poetry is an overflow or uprush of feeling which finds rhythmical form rather loosely in words, the words are then tied to and reinforced by the rhythm of music and dancing. The rhythm matters rather more

154

than the words. What that implies is not altogether difficult for us to comprehend. After all, in our own rather debased way, songs, dance tunes, and dances are combined. As we dance and as the hunchbacked and dinner-jacketed vocalist sings from the platform and as we sing with him, the rhythm matters rather more than the relation of the words. Or go from the dance hall into the Albert Hall for mass religion. The Foursquare Gospellers in London publish, or did publish before the war, a booklet of Elim choruses. Many of them read with the repetitive simplicity of primitive lyrics as the anthropologists record them. One of these choruses for Foursquare Gospelling multitudes may be simply a twelve-fold repetition of the one word 'Hallelujah' in groups of three; or it may be as simple as these two examples:

> I have an int'rest in the bleeding Lamb
> I have an int'rest in the bleeding Lamb
> I have an int'rest in the bleeding Lamb
> The Lamb of Calvary.

> He's the Lily of the Valley
>   To my soul
> He's the Lily of the Valley
>   To my soul.

> He's the Altogether Lovely
>   To my soul
> He's the Altogether Lovely
>   To my soul.

In one of their collections of the songs of jungle peoples in India, Verrier Elwin and Shamrao Hivale give a song which they translate:

> Hark to the song of the grasshopper,
> How ugly to look at,
> How sweet to hear.
> In which month sings the bird of sin?
> In which months sings the grasshopper?

It is a song which goes with a particular kind of dance. The people sing it very vigorously and quickly 'while their feet move in intricate rhythm', and they say that once they are caught by this dance 'they are lost to the world and all its troubles are forgotten'. Without the added rhythm of music and dancing, the rhythm of these words, just said, could not affect them in that degree.

With writing and civilization, this dancing of the rhythm drops out, leaving song—the poem with the music. To-day, in the Maikal Hills in the Central Provinces of India, the dance is dying out with the impact of civilization on the primitive peoples, and the song remains. Verrier Elwin reports that the dance songs 'are already being sung by the fireside or by lover to lover in bed rather than on the public dance ground'. So it goes on: the next stage, as a literature in our sense begins to develop, is to drop the music, as well as the dancing. Only the poem is left. All the while, poetry, as Yeats maintained, being 'an elaboration of the rhythms of common speech and their association with profound feeling'—the rhythm enters, or should enter, more and more strongly into the words. The dance and the music enter into the words; and there they must stay if the poem is to be a poem.

Obviously it is a very elementary mistake to interest oneself in primitive art, or so far as it has been studied in primitive poetry, and to conclude at once that the primitive establishes the universal norm. The digging-stick of neolithic agriculture develops into the multiple plough drawn by a tractor, but the function of the digging-stick continues in the plough. A dug-out has not to remain a dug-out, and there is a good case for it becoming an Irish curragh or an eight-oared racing-boat at Hammersmith, or a motor launch or a liner. The necessary thing, though, is that it should still float, however much it is elaborated. And in this situation the floating is the rhythm. As music and song have dropped away from the words, I repeat, as poetry has developed its autonomy, so it has in fact become all the more essential, if the poems are to be as fully effective as they can be, to strengthen the ryhthm in the words themselves, in the poems themselves.

I once saw a broadcast script by St. John Ervine about Arnold Bennett. One sentence lay innocently on the paper, like this, so far as I remember: 'Arnold even liked millionaire newspaper proprietors.' But in saying it St. John Ervine added to the sense, to the emotional and intellectual effect. It became something like this: 'Arnold—even *liked*'—then slowly and deliberately,

mouthing the consonants—'millionaire newspaper proprietors.'
The contempt, the spaced out contempt for the millionaires, was
magnificent. But all depended not on the arrangement of the
words on the paper. How then do you fix a poem so that the
words must be said just so by all readers who interpret the poem
rightly? By the *ars poetica* of contriving rhythmical constructions
out of language. What the poem carries or what the poem is can
be direct and simple, or it can be extremely complex. It can be
like that song from 'The Tragedy of Valentinian', when the
emperor comes in sick, in a chair:

> Care charming sleep, thou easer of all woes,
> Brother to death, sweetly thy self dispose
> On this afflicted Prince, fall like a cloud
> In gentle show'rs, giving nothing that is loud,
> Or painful to his slumbers; easy, sweet,
> And as a purling stream, thou son of night,
> Pass by his troubled senses; sing his pain
> Like hollow murmuring wind, or silver rain,
> Into this Prince gently, oh gently slide,
> And kiss him into slumbers like a bride.

The poem can be simple, like that, or complex, like:

> 'Tis the year's midnight, and it is the day's,
> Lucy's, who scarce seven hours herself unmaskes.
> The sun is spent, and now his flasks
> Send forth light squibs, no constant rays;
> The world's whole sap is sunk:
> The general balm th' hydroptic earth hath drunk
> Whither, as to the bed's feet, life is shrunk,
> Dead and enterr'd; yet all these seem to laugh
> Compar'd with me, who am their epitaph.
>
> Study me then, you who shall lovers be
> At the next world, that is at the next spring:
> For I am every dead thing,
> In whom love wrought new Alchemie.
> For his art did express
> A quintessence even from nothingness,
> From dull privations, and lean emptiness:
> He ruin'd me, and I am re-begot
> Of absence, darkness, death; things which are not.

Listening to those two complex stanzas (they are the beginning of Donne's 'Nocturnal on St. Lucy's Day') you could scarcely puzzle out the sense. You need the page for that, but you can get from its strong rhythms its emotional effectiveness straight away. It is an eye and an ear poem.

On the analogy of the dug-out and its inevitable elaboration, it seems obvious that the poet in our civilization most to be respected will, at all levels, have this rhythmical power over the combination of words, but will not always or rather all the time be content with the simpler and lower levels. Poetry once more is not so entirely a welling up of images or a presentation of verbal shocks as the establishment of words upon an emotionally compelling rhythm. Keep that—and it is here that the study of vernacular poetry, ballads, folk songs, street ballads, Elim choruses, popular songs, and primitive poetry, so far as that is accessible to us, is so useful—keep and intensify this rhythmical basis, and the dug-out can safely become the most complex ship on the water.

In English poetry for the last four hundred years the writers in the literate and educated tradition have constantly refreshed themselves from the vernacular, oral, uneducated tradition with its strong rhythmical simplicities. Mr. Eliot's example interrupted this interchange between the two traditions, for a while; Mr. Eliot and the Eliotizing poets have had a sympathy—rather too academic a sympathy—for decently composed and recorded literature of special kinds which could be boiled down into a somewhat free verse; but they have displayed next to no sympathy for that fertilizing and highly rhythmical vernacular and lyrical strain. So in my opinion English verse, true to its real nature, true to the nature of poetry, steps around the poems of Eliot and proceeds rather by Yeats and Hardy to Auden, and from Auden to the poets around him and after him. T. S. Eliot used to beg the question by saying that no verse was free for the man who wanted to do a good job. Herbert Read begged it by affirming that poetry was sincerity and had 'no essential alliance with regular schemes of any sort'. But observe how, unlike Chaucer, Dryden, Shakespeare, Tennyson, Yeats, or Mr. Auden, neither Mr. Eliot nor Mr. Read, for example, have displayed in their gifts any gift at all for lyricism. They were finding universal reasons to explain particular limits. No, on the long evidence, historical and physiological, I believe the best poet is, and will always be, at once capable of thinking in rhythmical form and of feeling in rhythmical form, at once capable of sustained length and of curtailed lyric—or limerick. His lyrical power, implying marked skill in rhythm and so in form, will be always the condition of his intellectual elaborations. The *ars poetica* goes between two poles of danger: one is an insistence upon a word-clogged and merely rhythmical poetry which reduces intellect, the other is an insistence upon an intellectualized poetry which reduces rhythm. For our civilization neither is a viable absolute.

Third Programme, 1949

26

THE LANGUAGE OF POETRY

I AM SPEAKING to-night of the art of contriving rhythmical constructions out of good language. Wordsworth—we may as well begin with Wordsworth—wrote about poetic diction that 'the earliest poets of all nations generally wrote from passion excited by real events; they wrote naturally, and as men: feeling powerfully as they did, their language was daring and figurative'. But he went on that in succeeding times: 'Poets, and Men ambitious of the fame of Poets, perceiving the influence of such language, and desirous of producing the same effect without being animated by the same passion, set themselves to a mechanical adoption of these figures of speech.'

'The earliest poets of all nations generally wrote from passion excited by real events'—back beyond writing, or alongside writing, that would be true as well. Let me illustrate this with two examples. The anthropologist Verrier Elwin says that the aboriginals whose songs he has collected in the Central Provinces of India sometimes will compose a song, a new song, in the excitement and rapture of dancing; and before they know what has happened the new song has become a public treasure. Franz Boas writes of a young Eskimo who was carried away on the drifting ice and did not manage to get back to land for several days: so, in his extreme danger, he made a song about himself and his situation. He repeated the song when he got home. The song appealed to everyone and 'soon became popular in all the villages'. We cannot imagine that Verrier Elwin's aboriginal or Franz Boas's Eskimo composed his words in any language except a natural language. But after many centuries of written and printed literature, it becomes, as it has become for us, difficult to avoid unnatural language, difficult, so it appears, to recognize the unnatural when we hear it or read it. How many times have we seen it stated within the last two years that Mr. Churchill is always a master of language, either in speech or in his books?

Three weeks ago Mr. Churchill complained in the House about the Supplementary Estimates:

'Mr. Morrison presumably realizes that we cannot wait for the indefinite delaying processes which the Prime Minister has employed. If these abuses are prolonged unduly, it will be necessary to raise the matter in the House if the elaborate procedure behind which the right honourable gentleman is sheltering himself is not yet exhausted.'

Unnatural language, because Mr. Churchill, in book or in speaking, knows too much about Ciceronian English, about Gibbon and Burke, and about the parliamentary orotundities of the last two hundred years; whereas Lloyd George, far nearer to the people and to the passionate oratory of Welsh pulpits, not educated at the best schools, far less nurtured on leading articles of *The Times*, was metaphorically more vivid and natural in his speeches. He once spoke about housing and how a man in Wales had to ride on his bicycle many miles to his work and back, morning and evening; he went on: 'I tell you if that man was a horse, you would build him a stable.'

Quite lately Sir Ernest Gowers, a civil servant who took a first in the Classical Tripos at Cambridge, wrote a pamphlet (called *Plain Words*) against official English; hardly a paragraph from end to end of the pamphlet, which was generally praised, is plain or free of the very unnatural and second-hand faults of diction which Sir Ernest Gowers hoped he was exposing. So I gather that Sir Ernest Gowers and Mr. Churchill do not listen to the lively speech of those who are less well educated than themselves. They have not an ear for such a remark as I heard from a man in a Wiltshire village. He was talking about a small husband and a large wife: 'If he said a word to her, she'd shrivel him up and poke him in a mouse-hole.' Not put him in a mouse-hole, but because he was now minute and shrivelled,—poke him into a mouse-hole, where he would be an easy fit.

Clearly it is a part of the *ars poetica* to listen to this common speech rather than the formalized speech of parliamentarians who will 'have to raise the matter in the House if the elaborate procedure behind which the right honourable gentleman is sheltering himself is not yet exhausted'. We can learn something more about the authenticity of poetic speech, as Mr. Owen Barfield once explained, from

> Thlee-piecee-bamboo, two-piecee puff-puff,
> walk-along-inside, no-can-see—

which is the pidgin English for a three-masted screw steamer with two funnels.

The trouble is mannerism, the persistence of dead modes of expression, partly because of our much clearer historical view of the past. Obviously all the arts are affected by this mannerism, notably architecture. Every so often, it is a commonplace to say, there is a poetic rebellion as the mode of the last rebellion becomes fixed and false, a rebellion or a slide back to a naturalism of speech. But then you must have such a naturalism of speech; and it is true that now the everyday speech of the middle and upper classes is more thoroughly smooth and tainted and lifeless than it ever has been. Indeed, the taint of the everyday speech of the educated also reduces the liveliness of the everyday speech of the less educated; and I think it true that the run of poetic speech from the eighteen-forties right down to 1949 has been more thoroughly tainted than ever before in English literature. Many of us are altogether insensitive to its bad qualities, and downstairs, in the prose department, we are also universally deaf to the use of dead metaphor in acquired rhythms. I beg you, if you are under the hypnosis of great names and great public achievements, to wake up and analyse coldly for yourself much of the received writing of our day, in prose and in verse, by public men, by novelists, by poets, by critics from Oxford and critics from Cambridge. Time will take care of such books; but our insensitive and sentimental acceptance of them as literature, or good writing, makes it even more essential, in the art of poetry, not only to employ language prompted in the authentic way by powerful feelings; but to listen—to listen as part of the basis for poetic speech, to the authentic everyday speech which is still current.

The relation of everyday speech to poetic speech was described best by Gerald Manley Hopkins, when he wrote that 'the poetical language of an age should be the current language heightened, to any degree heightened and unlike itself but not (I mean normally:

passing freaks and graces are another thing) an obsolete one. This is Shakespeare's and Milton's practice, and the want of it will be fatal to Tennyson's idylls and plays, to Swinburne and perhaps to Morris.' Several poets in the last century observed what was happening then to common and to poetic language. Hopkins was one, William Barnes was another, but still, even now, we have not thoroughly absorbed and put into practice their teachings on the matter. Social influences make it impossible, perhaps. I spoke last week about the rhythmical advantages to the *ars poetica* of studying (as such poets as Yeats and Auden and Louis MacNeice have done or poets did before them, such as Shakespeare and Dryden) the poems, chiefly songs, in the oral traditions of the vernacular. The advantages are verbal as well as rhythmical.

It is astonishing—the reason partly is reaction against reaction —to observe how much of the inferior verse of the nineteenth century we still accept, still praise in text-books, still force uncritically on the attention of schoolchildren and undergraduates. Now even Tennyson's wonderful melodic embroidery is contrived out of the artificial silks of language; and yet concurrently with his poems and with the soft mannerism of Victorian verse by other poets there existed or persisted a crude yet honest kind of poem, the street ballad. These ballads were contrived sometimes on old models or partly out of old materials by illiterate men for a few pennies a time, printed at Seven Dials and hawked around the streets.

> I'm a broken-hearted Gardener, and don't know what to do,
> My love she is inconstant, and a fickle jade, too,
> One smile from her lips will never be forgot,
> It refreshes like a shower from a watering-pot.
> > Oh, oh! She's a fickle wild rose,
> > A damask, a cabbage, a young China Rose.
>
> She's my myrtle, my geranium.
> My sunflower, my sweet marjoram,
> My honey-suckle, my tulip, my violet,
> My holly-hock, my dahlia, my mignonette.
>
> We grew up together like two apple trees,
> And clung to each other like double sweet peas,
> Now they're going to trim her, and plant her in a pot,
> And I'm left to wither, neglected and forgot.

She's my snow-drop, my ranunculus,
My hyacinth, my gillyflower, my polyanthus,
My heart's ease, my pink water-lily,
My buttercup, my daisy, my daffydown dilly.

I'm like a scarlet runner that has lost its stick,
Or a cherry that's left for the dickey to pick,
Like a water-pot I weep, like a paviour I sigh,
Like a mushroom I'll wither, like a cucumber, die.

I'm like a humble bee that doesn't know where to settle,
And she's a dandelion and a stinging nettle,
My heart's like a beetroot choked with chickweed,
And my head's like a pumpkin running to seed.

I've a great mind to make myself a felo-de-se,
And finish all my woes on the branch of a tree;
But I won't, for I know at my kicking you'd roar,
And honour my death with a double encore.
   Oh, oh! She's a fickle wild rose,
   A damask, a cabbage, a young China Rose.

It is naïve; but in language how direct and honest—'I'm like a scarlet runner that has lost its stick'!

How direct, how honest verbally, even syntactically you can see if you put 'The Broken-hearted Gardener' next to a love sonnet—rather a good sonnet—by Dante Gabriel Rossetti:

Your hands lie open in the long fresh grass,—
   The finger-points look through like rosy blooms:
   Your eyes smile peace. The pasture gleams and gleams
'Neath billowing skies that scatter and amass
All round our nest; far as the eye can pass,
   Are golden kingcup-fields with silver edge
   Where the cow-parsley skirts the hawthorn hedge.
'Tis visible silence, still as the hour-glass.

Deep in the sun-searched growths the dragon fly
Hangs like a blue thread loosened from the sky:—
   So this wing'd hour is dropt to us from above.
Oh! clasp we to our hearts for deathless dower,
This close-companioned inarticulate hour
   When two-fold silence was the song of love.

No, it does not quite do: that clasping 'to our hearts for death-less dower' doesn't do. It is not 'daring and figurative language', it is, in fact, Wordsworth's 'mechanical adoption' of old figures of speech. I repeat the odd thing is the endurance of such language even now. I could find it for you scarcely altered in the poems of several admired poets of our own day who are still under forty-five. How much more poetically exciting to us, after all, is that

> Thlee-piecee-bamboo, two-piecee puff-puff,
> walk-along-inside, no-can-see!

Other Victorian poets who escape enfeebled emotional language are the writers of nonsense. You cannot write effective nonsense in a dead mode of expression. So for good language again, how do these compare—Carroll and Swinburne, poets of two poems about love—nonsense love and nonsense love perhaps of another kind? Here are the two stanzas of Lewis Carroll:

> King-fisher courted Lady Bird—
> *Sing Beans, sing Bones, sing Butterflies!*
>   'Find me my match,' he said,
>   'With such a noble head—
> With such a beard, as white as curd—
>   With such expressive eyes!'

> 'Yet pins have heads,' said Lady Bird—
> *Sing Prunes, sing Prawns, sing Primrose-Hill!*
>   'And where you stick them in
>   They stay and thus a pin
> Is very much to be preferred
>   To one that's never still! . . .'

And Swinburne:

> Till death hath broken
> Sweet life's love-token,
> Till all be spoken
>   That shall be said,
> What dost thou praying,
> O soul, and playing
> With song and saying,
>   Things flown and fled?

For this we know not—
That fresh springs flow not—
And fresh griefs grow not
  When men are dead;
When strange years cover
Lover and lover
And joys are over
  And tears are shed.

Can we wonder that after mediaevalism and a poetic language like soft bars of chocolate, the satirists and the parodists became sharp?

She left her tower, and wandered down
Into the High Street of the town.
    O miserie!

Her pale feet glimmered, in and out,
Like tombstones as she went about.
    O miserie!

From right to left and left to right;
And blue veins streakt her instep white;
    O miserie!

And folks did ask her in the street
'How fared it with her long pale feet?'
    O miserie!

Victorian poetic language and our own version of it to-day arise from living too much within literature, too much out of the objective world from which figures may be derived. We as subjects are separated from everything outside ourselves as objects; we are no longer easily at home in the world, a situation which dulls the senses and dullens and smoothes out the language we use, or makes us use a language uncorrected and unenriched by sense impressions.

The aboriginals in India studied by Verrier Elwin make no subject-object division, absolutely, between themselves and their world, so their poetic language is figurative to a degree, even for songs which go with dancing. The necessary thing for a poet is to go on feeling colour as colour and not as wave-length, one is tempted to say. The necessary thing for him is to be rather more primitive in preserving the fineness of his sensations and in not withdrawing from perceptual reality, rather less civilized, rather more inclined to individualize and rather less to socialize his language. Hopkins, remember, said that the poetical language of an age should be not the current language, but the current language heightened. He heightened it himself to an extraordinary degree, partly through scholarship and knowledge of his own and diverse literatures, partly because he was like Dryden, who was not ashamed, so he said, 'to learn something about language from sailors', partly because he made language answer to the altogether unusual keenness of his perceptual powers, partly or mostly because passionate feeling induced a correspondingly passionate choice and combination of words. He delighted in technical terms out of agriculture, or sailing, or craftsmanship of any kind. Let me provide an example. His perceptual powers were so great that having long studied sunsets and made himself familiar with all the normal variations of light and colour in evening skies, he could at once detect and describe minutely and accurately all the difference in the evening skies caused in 1883 by that dust sent into the upper atmosphere when Krakatoa so violently erupted. In a letter to *Nature*, Hopkins wrote that an ordinarily bright sunset lines the clouds 'so that their brims look like gold, brass, bronze, or steel. It fetches out those dazzling flecks or spangles which people call fish-scales. It gives to a mackerel or dappled cloudrack the appearance of quilted crimson silk, or a ploughed field glazed with crimson ice', whereas the Krakatoa sunsets are distinguished by an intense glow which was also lustreless. 'It bathes', so he said, 'the whole sky, it is mistaken for the reflection of a great fire; at the sundown itself and southwards from that on December 4, I took a note of it as more like inflamed flesh than the lucid reds of ordinary sunsets. On the same evening the fields facing west glowed as if overlaid with yellow wax.'

If your senses apprehend with such intensity the evanescent colours in a sunset, they will answer verbally and rhythmically to all the colours of a passionate religious emotion. So I incline to believe that those who dislike Hopkins do so because they are limited in the intensity and the range of their own feelings and because they interpret that limit as conscious control. Hopkins is passionately in love with language. He is a passionate lover unusually alert to rhythms, unusually able to devise flawlessly strong and subtle effects of metre. Let us agree there is a 'too-muchness' in Hopkins, yet one reason for his celebration as a poet, let us also agree, is that his poetic language, so emphatically heightened and transparently justified, appeals to writers at a time when poetic language tends to paleness and anaemia and to feeble, intermittent pulsation of common educated speech. I maintain that just by his exaggerations, just by his too-muchness, Hopkins clarifies the nature and function and components of an authentic and heightened poetical language; his practice may not be imitable, but it proves how much the poetic language owes to the man and his perceptual nature, how much to the awareness of current speech, how much to literature critically observed.

If I said that so much Victorian badness of poetic language still survives, or a badness of poetic language closely kin to the Victorian, we can also claim that in spite of all the difficulties there has been enough of the art of contriving rhythmical constructions out of good language to give us a poetic language of our own age, well founded and well heightened upon occasion. Do you remember the name of Clere Parsons, a poet who died when he was twenty-three, in 1931? Mr. Eliot was partly responsible for publishing a selection of his poems after his death. One poem was 'Suburban Nature Piece'. It exemplifies this poetic language of our time, heightened considerably and rhythmically in close control, it is in the new language, but it mocks the old poetic language out of which it emerges:

> April who dost abet me with shy smiles
> If I made bold by amorous fancy touch
> Suddenly with my lips thy shining lips which
> Are the smooth tulip and chaste crocus bulb
> Lady be swift to pardon me this much
>
> This day cannot long delay his choice between
> Whether to be spring or remain winter still
> —Behold the impetuous sun flings light like scarves
> Of petalled lace to dazzle the ocean and
> With silver lance our wintry moods to kill

THE LANGUAGE OF POETRY

Sweet month thou dost incite me to review
My fearful ship that hath all hopes in hold
O august barque of destiny bear me on
Safely those difficult and deep tides to where
No bird of fire shall steal my apples of gold

Throw open portholes and notice how the in-
Curved water at our wake is making a green
Drain smooth as glass but it must break
As the present breaks vanishing into the past
Pretending there the gayest days have been

(Which is exactly not what either I
Or you really believe rather I swear
We begin here and now and shall throw no
Elegant flowers to sobbing yesterdays
We are not yet collected works my dear)

Hail early nervous lucent appearing veil
Of tiniest veined leaf weaving a screen
To hide the bare and winter-weary black
Boles of the sentinel dejected trees
Wood ways shall soon be smelling earthy-clean

And here is the generous almond tree whose pink
Victorian skirt primly resists the wind
The ice-cream man who stands by the park gate
Is lifting towards the sun his commonplace
Simian face which is evil and grey-skinned

For with warm days also his trade revives
The children come with fixed and longing eyes
And with saved pennies as often as they can
To savour the small inverted cones of white
Ice cream surely consumed in Paradise

Amiable month unglove thy lovely hand
And with soft fingers conjure from the waste
Barren dry desolate sandstone of the mind
And stagnant pools of stale and weary thought
Rich water-lilies lightly to be embraced

THE LANGUAGE OF POETRY

By rainbow-tailed delirious dragon-flies
Whose arrowing vivid sudden amazing flight
In summer stings the quiet bowls of shade
Bestirred by thee my thoughts again shall dive
Into remote space like violet rays of light

Listen my dears the skies are going out
Moonlight shall bathe the sleeping nenuphars
Musicians bring forth your violas-da-gamba
And stab my heart with bronze chords now that night
Gently is brushing the alarmed sky with stars.

A good poem, admirably contrived, I hope you will agree, of rhythmic subtlety and form—admirably heightened out of daily speech, and heightened mockingly, as I say, out of the older poetic speech, even to its falsities. It was near the beginning of an extent of English poetry going across the next seventeen years and including fearless poems of a remarkable nature, and a remarkable richness, and strength of rhythm and strength of language; by one or two poets, let me remind you, who have not yet come to middle age, and are still perfecting their own art of poetry.

Third Programme, 1949

27

THE ENJOYMENT OF POETRY

(A Broadcast to Sixth Forms, 1947)

SUPPOSE BROADCASTING had existed at the time of Shakespeare, Chaucer, Virgil, Homer; suppose there had been broadcasts about poetry, no one would ever have thought it necessary to broadcast about the *enjoyment* of poetry.

I meant to choose a title which suggested that poems—reading poems—was as natural and normal a pleasure as playing chess or going to the movies. For example, I avoided 'The Meaning of Poetry'. I aimed to avoid anything implying that poetry had to be explained, defined, or excused. But it is no good. What was a normal enjoyment for many or most of us, what has been a normal enjoyment, no doubt, from the English Stone Age, all through the primitive and less primitive cultures and through all the greatest times of humanity, has become an enjoyment for fewer and fewer educated people; so even an innocent title like 'The Enjoyment of Poetry' suggests that some of you perhaps do not enjoy it all, suggests that what I have to do is to argue you into thinking that poetry, after all, is not the bunk. And of course you could find high support for thinking that it is the bunk. If you are a scientist, and not a classicist, and if that is how you stand to poetry, you have Sir Isaac Newton on your side. He was asked what he thought of poetry. He replied that it was 'an ingenious piece of nonsense'. Darwin, when he was mature, lost, he said, 'all pleasure from poetry of any kind, including Shakespeare', though he had the grace to say that he had done so to his great regret. To go a bit further back, between Newton and Darwin, George III thought nothing of poetry. When Alexander Pope was famous, he remarked—or so it is said— 'Who is this Pope that I hear so much about? I cannot discover what is his merit. Why will not my subjects write in prose?' His subjects' descendants do mostly write in prose. Eighty years ago Mr. Gladstone ruled England in intervals between reading Homer. Between the wars Mr. Baldwin ruled England in intervals between reading the novels—the prose—of Mary Webb. A split began at some time, dividing men into the practical man and the poetic man, between, in two words that H. G. Wells introduced into English, highbrow and lowbrow; and Sir Isaac Newton lived when that split was just beginning to be obvious. In a way, and at that moment, science and philosophy were to blame. There is a good short statement about this in the book which Professor Raven had just published—*English Naturalists from Neckham to Ray*, which he also names 'A study in the making of the modern world'. The naturalists, the new scientists, began to measure, number, and name the objects and the creatures of the world, to be doubtful about accepted views, to demolish mediaeval notions such as the notion that an elephant has no bones, or that a bear licks its shapeless new-born cubs into shape. If verifying and investigating by exact methods was under way, then what was to happen when man, and his God, his religion, all that he believed supernaturally, as well as nature, as well as boneless elephants, came under this new exact scrutiny?

How was the opposition of the Church, and if you like, of the poets, to be avoided? The answer, given by the philosopher Descartes, was to divide, to split, to put mankind and the supernatural on one side, to leave them more or less alone, to group all other things, and everything else that lived, on the other side, for scientists to examine and weigh and measure.

It was very neat. It was very necessary to science and to the making of the modern world; but it was dangerous for that world, for you and me, and Darwin and Lord Baldwin and nuclear physicists developing the atom bomb. At the time it did mean that a man could be a scientist and a clergyman with a good conscience, a parish priest and a Fellow of the Royal Society; could preach his sermon on Sunday morning, like the Rev. Dr. Hales, F.R.S., and then hurry back to his garden where a white horse was tied to a gate, where parson Hales opened its carotid artery, inserted a glass tube, and proved that the pressure in the artery would force the blood in the tube up to so many feet and so many inches. But as Professor Raven says, all this also meant 'that science would confine itself to the sphere of weight and measurement, that biological, psychological and religious studies would be distorted'; it meant a radical split of a kind 'which would have disastrous effects upon human welfare'. It meant that there would be two interpretations and not a unified interpretation of the universe. It meant that you and I, before very long, together with Darwin and Newton, might not be enjoying poetry, that very likely we might all be despising it as ingenious nonsense, and coming to think everything material and verifiable much more valuable than everything immaterial, unverifiable, and spiritual.

So, a hundred years or so later, a poet and painter such as Blake, who stands for the immaterial and the divine, depicted Newton as a naked, atheistical devil, sitting on material rocks, and measuring material with a pair of dividers. So Blake writes a poem against material-measuring, against science as the highest value:

> Mock on, mock on Voltaire, Rousseau:
> Mock on, Mock on: 'tis all in vain!
> You throw the sand against the wind,
> And the wind blows it back again.
>
> And every sand becomes a Gem
> Reflected in the beams divine;
> Blown back they blind the mocking Eye,
> But still in Israel's paths they shine.
>
> The Atoms of Democritus
> And Newton's Particles of light
> Are sands upon the Red Sea shore,
> When Israel's tents do shine so bright.

Now let me say what poems actually do. By way of material things, by words, by words symbolic of things or creatures, a sunflower if you like, a diamond, a broken bedstead, or a chipped teapot with a yellow spout, a girl in a blue dress or a witch on a blasted heath, by this way of the material poems deal with the immaterial; they deal with everything in our lives, as people, as human beings who feel and think, which cannot be easily measured, verified, labelled, and explained. From those experiences none of us are altogether free—unless we are mentally defective. We feel at times, for no particular obvious reason, that everything around us, say on a clear evening in May, at 7 o'clock, is sparklingly and peculiarly lovely, and that we are part of that loveliness. We dive into water, swim and walk out on the sand, are delighted by the feel of our bodies and a sense of ease; we fall in love; we are religious and feel an intense love of the divine. All these are experiences which can be concentrated and fixed by us, or for us, in poems. Something delights us by being incongruous or funny. Something moves us by being terrible or tragic. Someone we love does not love us. Someone good and innocent is overwhelmed and destroyed through his own errors or through other men's evil. We are assailed by delightful or terrible dreams. We are aware that somebody or something is mean, brutal, vile, or conceited in his own stupidity. Again, all of these are experiences which find words out of which poems are made.

Perhaps, before us, our friends have to die, our children, our parents, our wives; we have to die ourselves. Death, like life, is one of the great constant subjects for poetry, whether we feel that death is an end, or an entrance, an entrance into splendour, or an end which is dismal and black like the end of the heroes in the *Iliad*. Some of these inevitable experiences we wish to celebrate and enjoy. In some of them we need consolation and strength. Some are trivial, some are overwhelmingly serious, so the poems into which they are *condensed* vary from the witty or the light and pleasant to the immense—from Geoffrey Taylor's 'Cruel Clever Cat' to the immense end of a tragedy by Shakespeare or the ritual free verse of *The Order for the Burial of the Dead*:

> Sally having eaten cheese
> Puffs down the hole the scented breeze
> Enticing thus with baited breath
> Nice mice to an untimely death.

'Man that is born of a woman hath but a short time to live, and is full of misery. He cometh up, and is cut down, like a flower; he fleeth as it were a shadow and never continueth in one stay. In the midst of life we are in death . . .'

Put two more side by side, a delicate rather sad lyric written by a highly sensitive, lonely, stuttering Irishman, George Darley, which is called 'The Mermaiden's Vesper Hymn':

Troop home to silent grots and caves!
Troop home! And mimic as you go
The mournful winding of the waves
Which to their dark abysses flow!

At this sweet hour, all things beside
In amorous pairs to covert creep;
The swans that brush the evening tide
Homeward in snowy couples keep;

In his green den the murmuring seal
Close by his sleek companion lies;
While singly we to bedward steal
And close in fruitless sleep our eyes.

In bowers of love men take their rest,
In bowers of love we sigh alone!
With bosom-friends are others blest,—
But we have none! but we have none!

Suggestive, melancholy, sweet poetry of the sweet hour—yes, but then, from Dryden's translation of Juvenal's sixth satire, try the tremendous precise hardness which is also in poems:

In Saturn's reign, at Nature's early birth,
There was that thing called Chastity on earth;
When in a narrow cave, their common shade
The sheep, the shepherds, and their Gods were laid:
When reeds and leaves, and hides of beasts were spread
By mountain huswifes for their homely bed,
And mossy pillows raised, for the rude husband's head.
Unlike the niceness of our modern dames,
(Affected nymphs with new affected names)
The *Cynthias* and the *Lesbias* of our years,
Who for a sparrow's death dissolve in tears,
Those first unpolished matrons, big and bold,
Gave suck to infants of gigantic mould,
Rough as their savage lords who rang'd the wood,
And fat with acorns belcht their windy food.

Terrific—terrific and masculine; as George Darley's swans in snowy couples and seals in the green den were feminine and delicate. Or it might be better to say Darley's poem is tender,

Dryden's lines are tough. I am aiming to show at the moment the variety of poems in response to the variety of our needs, which are liable to be different, say when we get up, or before we go to bed; the variety of poems we can enjoy, and not—I shall need to say something of that—the factor which makes all of them into poems. And one poet, just as one reader, varies in his knowledge and his mood. I hope you read Thomas Hardy. Hardy was in the main a grave, sad poet; but always honest. When the first great war ended, Hardy sent an Armistice Day poem to *The Times*. This is part of it:

> Breathless they paused. Out there men raised their glance
> To where had stood those poplars lank and lopped,
> As they had raised it through the four years' dance
> Of Death in the now familiar flats of France;
> And murmured: 'Strange, this! How? All firing stopped?'
>
> Aye; all was hushed. The about-to-fire fired not,
> The aimed-at moved away in trance-lipped song.
> One checkless regiment slung a clinching shot
> And turned. The Spirit of Irony smirked out, 'What?
> Spoil peradventures woven of Rage and Wrong?'
>
> Thenceforth no flying fires inflamed the grey,
> No hurtlings shook the dewdrop from the thorn,
> No moan perplexed the mute bird on the spray;
> Worn horses mused: 'We are not whipped to-day';
> No weft-winged engines blurred the moon's thin horn.
>
> Calm fell. From Heaven distilled a clemency;
> There was peace on earth, and silence in the sky;
> Some could, some could not, shake off misery:
> The Sinister Spirit sneered: 'It had to be!'
> And again the Spirit of Pity whispered, 'Why?'

The same poet sat once in 1893 with a girl in a hansom cab:

> She wore a new terra-cotta dress,
> And we stayed, because of the pelting storm,
> Within the hansom's dry recess,
> Though the horse had stopped; yes, motionless
>   We sat on, snug and warm.

Then the downpour ceased, to my sharp sad pain
And the glass that had screened our forms before
Flew up, and out she sprang to her door:
I should have kissed her if the rain
　　　Had lasted a minute more.

You may think I am being very obvious, emphasizing that
Hardy, one poet, wrote those two poems of distinct mood, distinct
experience, and distinct application. Perhaps. But the greater
your poet, in every graduation, from Hardy up to Shakespeare,
the more variety there is in his poems, the more experiences he
illuminates, the more he satisfies our need as human beings. And
all of us, however less human we become, however more auto-
matic, however more unfeeling, are born human, whether we are
born in Virgil's century, or in Shakespeare's, or in this more
prosaic century which is not sure whether or not it does enjoy—
or need—poetry. There was a time early in Darwin's life, whatever happened afterwards, when he used to sit in a window and
read Shakespeare by the hour.

A broadcast on poetry in Shakespeare's day would have taken
the need, the enjoyment, for granted. Perhaps it would have been
a broadcast on the technique, on the skills of writing poetry, a
broadcast aimed at improving a fairly general habit. The broad-
caster would not have needed to name that common factor which
unites the variety of words conveying and condensing the variety
of experiences—which unites all the different species of poem and
poet into the one family called poetry. I should say of this
factor, with Dryden, that 'I am satisfied if it cause delight'; but
I should add with Dryden that 'poesy only instructs as it delights';
and with Coleridge I should qualify that delight as 'musical
delight'. The enjoyment of poetry is the enjoyment and comfort
of reading all the possible pleasures, exultations, sadnesses, and
tragedies, all the fundamental wisdom of men about men—all of
it variously condensed—I use that word again—and made by the
most honest arrangement of words into what is musical and
memorable. It is our reality as human beings who think and
feel, and believe that good is good and bad is bad; so given to us
that we can grasp it and have it working inside ourselves. It is
not against science, but at its highest it is material and spiritual,
the material of science and the spiritual mixed into one.

28

THE MAKING OF A POEM

THE POEM whose making I want to unpick and to place in its right sequence in a poet's life, his thoughts, and his tragedies, was written inside a lunatic asylum. It is not a very complicated, a very obscure, or a very long poem. The poet is John Clare. The poem:

> I lost the love of heaven above,
> I spurned the lust of earth below,
> I felt the sweets of fancied love,
> And hell itself my only foe,
>
> I lost earth's joys, but felt the glow
> Of heaven's flame abound in me,
> Till loveliness and I did grow
> The bard of immortality.
>
> I loved, but woman fell away,
> I hid me from her faded flame,
> I snatched the sun's eternal ray
> And wrote till earth was but a name.
>
> In every language upon earth,
> On every shore, o'er every sea,
> I gave my name immortal birth
> And kept my spirit with the free.

To understand how and why Clare wrote that, how he came to that ultimate, triumphant freedom, we have to go back from the Northampton asylum where he was confined into Clare's childhood.

Who was Clare? And how did Clare begin to write poems? And why? He was a farm-labourer's son, born in the village of Helpstone, in Northamptonshire, in 1793. A peculiar 'sport' biologically, born into a family with no particular distinction. He wrote, later on, a good many fragments of autobiography, and one of them describes everything which entertained him and held him in childhood—nearly always things that he saw. He observed, he says:

> 'the blue corn-bottles crowding their splendid colours in large sheets over the land and troubling their cornfields with destroying beauty: the different greens of the woodland trees, the dark oak, the paler ash, the mellow lime, the white poplars peeping above the rest like leafy steeples, the grey willow shining chilly in the sun, as if the morning mist still lingered on its cool green.'

And he carries on the catalogue, saying that 'he felt the beauty of all these with eager delight'. But 'I knew nothing of poetry. It was felt and not uttered.'

All these things he saw were the crude material of our madhouse poem; but the material, the experience, collected and absorbed before he could talk of snatching the sun's eternal ray and writing till earth became a name, and keeping his spirit with the free—all this material is the story of how life hit him in the face, the story of the joys that Clare had, and the slow, tragical way he came to discover what he thought was the meaning of life, and what were the things that mattered, in being a human being and sharing human life with other human beings. In the poem there is much about love—love of women—

> I loved, but woman fell away
> I hid me from her faded flame.

And in love there are many stages and complications. It begins narrowly and gets wider—loving parents, loving another person, loving all human beings, good and bad, till love can seem the one thing which makes sense of this hard business of being alive.

'I was a lover very early in life,' Clare says, in another scrap of his autobiography. 'My first attachment, being a schoolboy affection, was for Mary who was beloved with a romantic, or Platonic sort of feeling. . . . Her heart was as tender as a bird's. . . . I remember an accident that roused my best intentions, and hurt my affection into the rude feelings of imaginary cruelty. When playing one day in the churchyard I threw a green walnut that hit her on the eye. She wept, and I hid my sorrow and my affection together under the shame of not showing regret, lest others might laugh it into love.'

Now, at this stage, those sights he had seen and liked but not known exactly why, and this business of loving another person, discovering the existence of another person—these two concerns came together and mixed: things seen illustrated and became part of love; and so you get Clare writing an early poem, in which he talks about spring, about the hoarse crows finding 'softer notes for love', and which he ends by saying:

> The flowers join lips below, the leaves above,
> And every sound that meets the ear is love.

About Clare and this child Mary. He never married her. His love for her, so far as the direct sharing of life went, did not surpass that childish or Platonic affection. He fell in love with other women, he married another woman, and they had children. But, in fact, his love never shifted from that first person who had woken it up, who, in the body, had walked right out of his life. He went on loving her till she became for him not just physical love, or love of another person, but all love, the whole principle of love, loving everything, everybody, all that lives and exists— Clare's heavenly love.

> I lost earth's joys, but felt the glow
> Of heaven's flame abound in me,
> Till loveliness and I did grow
> The bard of immortality.

When he first showed signs of madness, they put him in an asylum in Epping Forest, but did not confine him very much. He was free to walk in the Forest. Here he wrote poems about love of women—love, in fact, of Mary. Then he felt he must go to this vanished, absent Mary. He walked off to look for her, walked miles with no money, no food, towards his village—a terrible journey (of which he wrote an exact description); which ended not by finding Mary, but by being picked up by his real wife in a pony cart.

Now in his childhood, watching flowers, insects, birds, trees, he had been, without knowing it, free. In Epping Forest, in the first asylum, though not shut up, he had lost his freedom; he

had been under restraint; and so by the loss of freedom, he became aware of freedom, he understood and felt that freedom was
a great necessity for him: freedom joined love, and those objects
of nature, which had already mixed with love.

There is a poem he wrote some time after that journey to find
Mary, which had been as terrible as Herman Melville's description
of walking on the rough bed of the sea after it had been 'left bare by
Faith's receding wave'. The poem talks to Mary as though she
was there with him. He picks flowers with her, and then finishes
up with this verse:

> Mary, or sweet spirit of thee,
> As the bright sun shines to-morrow,
> Thy dark eyes these flowers shall see
> Gathered by me in sorrow,
> In the still hour when my mind was free
> To walk alone—yet wish I walked with thee.

New things have entered in—he has developed further in life,
learned more of life's tricks. You would realize, if I read the
whole poem, how the old things are still there, felt still more
sharply and clearly—the things seen—the crescent moon reflected
in the water, the still, tender lake which he feels is actually pressed
by the path along the edge of it, the flowers, the dew, the love.
But life has given him two of the hits in the face: sorrow—

> Thy dark eyes these flowers shall see
> Gathered by me in sorrow—

and lack of freedom, knowledge of freedom—

> In the still hour when my mind was free
> To walk alone—yet wish I walked with thee.

But Clare as a poet had still to grow up. Take an obvious
image—seedling: in the seedling days 'I knew nothing of poetry.
It was felt and not uttered'; flower—the days of

> The flowers join lips below, the leaves above
> And every sound that meets the ear is love;

and seed, the climax of seedling and flower. Clare has not yet
grown to that climax; love, sorrow, freedom, are still (though

not entirely) personal—*his* love, *his* sorrow, *his* freedom. But in this last poem about Mary, the veined coloured petals are beginning to shrivel, and leave the seed naked and ready to grow in the world of the hearts of readers—of you and of me.

After Clare returned from his first asylum in that great walk, he was allowed to be free for a time—and live at home in his cottage at Helpstone with his wife and his children. Not for long. They took him away again, to the closer restraint of the county asylum at Northampton. He had paper there, and could write. He was allowed, for some years, to go down into the town and sit in the portico, day by day, of one of the churches. Sitting there this unconsidered and nearly forgotten madman saw the young Queen Victoria pass through Northampton on her Progress, in 1844.

Sometimes he thought he was Lord Byron, sometimes a champion boxer—both for him, Byron and the boxer, were fighters against the world's indifference, champions of freedom.

From the asylum, after his roaming was checked, he wrote a letter to his wife. Part of it goes:

'My dear Wife,

I have not written to you a long while, but here I am in the Land of Sodom where all the people's brains are turned the wrong way. I was glad to see John yesterday and should like to have gone back with him, for I am weary of being here. You might come and fetch me away, for I think I have been here long enough. I write this in a green meadow the side of the river, agen Stokes Mill, and I see three of your daughters and a son now and then. The confusion and roar of the Mill-dams and locks, is sounding very pleasant as I write it, and it's a very beautiful evening; the meadows are greener than usual after the shower, and the rivers are brimful. I think it is about two years since I was first sent up in this Hell and not allowed to go out of the gates. There never was a more disgraceful deception than this place . . . keep yourselves happy and love one another.'

Like the poem, you can take that letter to pieces. Nature—the objects he saw—still there; sorrow—still there. Freedom—still aware of it, still aware of its absence. Love—yes. Yet not just his love; but an order to others to love—'Love one another'.

What happens when the petals are right off, and the seed is left not merely sheer, by itself, but matured and ripened? Well, the poem by Clare we are taking to bits. The love that Clare reaches, shut up in the asylum, cut from his family, going into attitudes of defence and offence like a champion pug, may have begun as love of woman:

> I felt the sweets of fancied love,
> And hell itself my only foe.

But it has become love feeling out, speaking out through the world, loving all human beings, love like that of Blake (who believed) 'everything which lives is holy'; it is love making sense of life—and of death.

I take it from the first line of the poem,

> I lost the love of heaven above,

that Clare obscurely felt he had known, even if he had not recognized, this final, heavenly, flaming love as a boy, before the flame of women entered into his life and drove the heavenly love out of him—there is another poem which explains this flame of heaven, beginning

> Love lives beyond
> The tomb, the earth, which fades like dew!
> I love the fond,
> The faithful, and the true.

But in our particular poem, the point is less love than the final freedom of a love which reached above women, or flowers, or dew, or the crescent moon; not just Clare's freedom from the asylum, but the freedom Clare has reached entirely beyond the asylum as the Love was beyond the Earth. He wrote with the sun's ray—the ray of love, till earth, with its asylums, was only a name. He was free; but not only as an individual: he had joined the company of the free:

> I gave my name immortal birth
> And kept my spirit with the free.

So Clare, by the end, speaks for everybody's sorrow, everybody's freedom, everybody's love—he speaks for principles; and you will notice, if you read some of his last poems, how the natural objects of his early childhood have almost vanished, have been compressed into words like *green* and *dew* and *spring*; and how in this particular poem even the compressions of 'dew' and 'green', and so on, have vanished, leaving for those who can feel them big and naked words, *Love* and *Free*, to stand almost by themselves in the loveliness of the sound of the poem. But where did these bare words Love and Free start from? Still precisely from all the things he saw and felt as a child, from the blue cornbottles, the green walnut which he threw at the girl, the roundy sun rising over the fens. Precisely from these things, which have not merely dropped away, but are behind the words *Love* and *Free*, are there in them, in the way they are used.

You have then a poet who uses his eyes—and his ears—interestingly, and deepens the interest of his poetry as his own life changed and deepened.

As oil of lavender is the essence of a great mass of lavender piled up in a shed, so such a poem as ours is the end of a great mass of life. It is what a man writes who has a gift for putting words together musically and so that you can remember them, when his finger has touched the warmth of life and the satin chilliness of death.

Only those poets can write down bare words and notions like Love and Freedom so that we can feel them; only those poets who have worked their way with and through some of all the interesting things that lie about in the world for us to see, feel, hear. You cannot begin with those final words: you can only come to them through life as to the meaning of life—and so such a poet as Clare is a visionary: he is one whose eyes absorb life and leaves, and pass through them until they see into what they believe is the meaning of life. And for most poets that meaning of life becomes Love, or Love and Freedom. I think we must always distrust poetry and poets who try to reach the Large Words by a short cut. There are no short cuts, and the road to these words is long, awkward, badly surfaced, twisty, and roundabout. And perhaps it is worth mentioning that Chinese poets who have been most fond of teaching their audience in bare words about Good and Evil, good conduct of life and bad conduct of life nearly always offer their lessons in the solid imagery of trees, flowers, mountains—even modern Chinese poets who have deliberately fed from Europe and from such Europeans as Mr. Eliot and Mr. W. H. Auden.

This poem, then, of Clare's is the man's final staring into the eye of life.

Home Service, 1946

29

THOMAS CHATTERTON

THE TROUBLE with Chatterton is that there are two Chattertons. One is the poet, the Chatterton who exists in the poems. The other is the sensational Chatterton, the seventeen-year-old boy—who was a genius, as we say; who was misused by that in some ways nasty character Horace Walpole; who starved; who committed suicide in a London garret. It is, I agree, a wonderful, pathetic story. But the important Chatterton is the other one, the poet; and if Chatterton had been run over by a coach, or slipped on the stairs, or fallen into the river on a dark night, he would still be as important, he would still be worth reading, as a remarkable English poet.

All the same, I want to remind you of the scene of Chatterton's death, as it was imagined, very exquisitely, by the Pre-Raphaelite painter Henry Wallis. The picture is in the Tate Gallery. Chatterton lies dead under a small attic window, through which you can see St. Paul's. He wears breeches of a vivid satin blue. Red hair curls round a handsome face—the model for the picture, by the way, was another poet, George Meredith, with whose wife the painter disappeared. Near his feet a plum-coloured coat hangs over a chair. It is a very rich painting, a painting of richly combined colour; imagined, but true, in spite of somewhat sententious details which have to be 'read', because to my mind it symbolizes the richness and the colour of Chatterton's poetry.

> On Tiber's banks, where scarlet jasmines bloom,
> And purple aloes shed a rich perfume;
> Where, when the sun is melting in his heat,
> The reeking tigers find a cool retreat,
> Bask in the sedges, lose the sultry beam,
> And wanton with their shadows in the stream—

Chatterton is alert, like Keats, in more than one sense at the same time, vision and the senses of smell and touch. That is what I mean by Chatterton's colour and richness—scarlet jasmines mixed with scent and purple aloes, and tigers reeking in strong sunshine.

You will have seen a macaw at the zoo. Macaws can be scarlet and purple and green; they come from tropical South America; and macaws are a favourite bird in the tropics of Chatterton's poetry—as though he had seen macaws, as he well may have done, brought back on the quays of the Port of Bristol.

Here is one of Chatterton's macaw poems, which he called, not exactly knowing where macaws came from, 'An African Song':

> Haste, ye purple gleams of light,
>   Haste and gild the spacious skies;
> Haste, ye eagles, take your flight,
>   Haste and bid the morning rise.
>
> Now the Eastern curtain draws;
>   Now the red'ning splendour gleams,
> Now the purple plum'd maccaws
>   Skim along the silver streams.
>
> Now the fragrant-scented thorn,
>   Trembles with the gummy dew;
> Now the pleasures of the morn,
>   Swell upon the eager view.
>
> Whither does my archer stray?
>   Whither is my Narva fled?
> What can keep his soul away
>   From the transports of Mored?

All these African poems by Chatterton were written by him in London, in the last seven or eight months of his life; and I think they show his real bent, his real nature and peculiarity as a poet rather more than his famous Rowley Poems, his imitations—or imagined recreations—of Chaucerian English. The African poems are much less known, less read, and less admired, so I am going to take a longish piece from one of them, from 'Heccar and Gaira'; Heccar and Gaira are two warriors, and Heccar reminds Gaira of his wife Cawna and of the depredations of the pallid children of the wave, the slave traders—remember that Chatterton was a Bristolian and Bristol a slave traders' port:

'Rouse not remembrance from her shadowy cell'—

Gaira replies—

Nor of those bloody sons of mischief tell.
Cawna, O Cawna! decked in sable charms,
What distant region holds thee from my arms?
Cawna, the pride of Afric's sultry vales,
Soft as the cooling murmur of the gales;
Majestic as the many-coloured snake,
Trailing his glories through the blossomed brake;
Black as the glossy rocks, where Eascal roars,
Foaming through sandy wastes to Jaghir's shores;
Swift as the arrow, hasting to the breast,
Was Cawna, the companion of my rest.

The sun sat low'ring in the western sky,
The swelling tempest spread around the eye;
Upon my Cawna's bosom I reclined,
Catching the breathing whispers of the wind.
Swift from the wood a prowling tiger came,
Dreadful his voice, his eyes a glowing flame;
I bent the bow, the never-erring dart
Pierced his rough armour, but escaped his heart;
He fled, though wounded, to a distant waste,
I urged the furious flight with fatal haste;
He fell, he died—spent in the fiery toil,
I stripped his carcase of the furry spoil,
And, as the varied spangles met my eye,
'On this', I cried, 'shall my loved Cawna lie.'

The dusky midnight hung the skies in grey;
Impelled by love, I winged the airy way;
In the deep valley and the mossy plain,
I sought my Cawna, but I sought in vain.
The pallid shadows of the azure waves
Had made my Cawna, and my children, slaves.
Reflection maddens to recall the hour;
The gods had giv'n me to the demon's power.
The dusk slow vanished from the hated lawn,
I gained a mountain glaring with the dawn.
There the full sails, expanded to the wind,
Struck horror and distraction in my mind;
There Cawna, mingled with a worthless train,
In common slavery drags the hated chain.

> Now judge, my Heccar, have I cause for rage?
> Should aught the thunder of my arm assuage?
> In ever-reeking blood this javelin dyed
> With vengeance shall be never satisfied;
> I'll strew the beaches with the mighty dead
> And tinge the lily of their features red.

That last line—'And tinge the lily of their features red'—or that earlier line 'I gained a mountain glaring with the dawn'—it is the kind of grandeur, the kind of extravagance which Chatterton could produce again and again. Sometimes one or two lines like that come just when you think the poem is dull, silly, and underdone.

> Like snows that trickle down hot Ætna's steep.

There is another of his grand lines for the Avon at Bristol:

> And the full Avon lifts the darken'd wave.

Chatterton's poetry was not only drawn out of mediaevalism and the tropics—out of two distant countries, one in time and one in space which he had only imagined and never seen. The brilliant eyes which all Chatterton's friends remembered—his brilliant grey eyes, took in, gloomily and grandly, details of the autumn landscape at Bristol:

> The yellow Avon, creeping at my side,
> In sullen billows rolls a muddy tide;
> No sportive naiads on her streams are seen,
> No cheerful pastimes deck the gloomy scene.

Yellow was a favourite colour, a favourite adjective in Chatterton's mind. He writes in one of his Bristol poems, the 'Elegy to the Memory of Mr. Thomas Phillips':

> Here, stretched upon this heaven-ascending hill
> I'll wait the horrors of the coming night,
> I'll imitate the gently-plaintive rill,
> And by the glare of lambent vapours write.

Then the yellow line:

> Wet with the dew, the yellow Hawthornes bow;
> The loud winds whistle through the echoing dell;
> Far o'er the lea the breathing cattle low
> And the shrill shrieking of the screech-owl swell.

With whistling sound the dusky foliage flies,
  And wantons with the wind in rapid whirls;
The gurgling rivulet to the valley hies,
  And, lost to sight, in dying murmurs curls . . .

Chatterton played about with that poem, wrote and rewrote it.
One can see how his mind was made up, and how his mind worked,
from the changes. The gurgling rivulet curling out of sight in
dying murmurs suggested to him a snake, so he rewrote that last
stanza like this:

With rustling sound the yellow foliage flies—

yellow instead of *dusky*—

  And wantons with the wind in rapid whirls.
  The gurgling riv'let to the valley hies
  Whilst on the bank the spangled serpent curls.

In other words, there is one of Chatterton's tropical snakes
luxuriating in the coloured autumn of some stream side in Leigh
Woods; and there you see the furniture of Chatterton's mind.
You would find in it, if you could open the lid, a pretty strange
mixture—brown owls and scarlet macaws, Gothic ruins and
African jungles, knights in armour and black naked warriors
with high-sounding names, striped tigers and hot sunshine, yellow
leaves and autumn fogs, snakes and spices and volcanoes with
Bristol's muddy river rolling along to Avonmouth.

You have to add to that the pride, vigour, and intelligence of
Chatterton—the power to write strong lines of suggestive
mystery:

  On Tiber's banks where scarlet jasmines bloom,
  And purple aloes shed a rich perfume;
  Where, when the sun is melting in his heat,
  The reeking tigers find a cool retreat.

It is such lines, or lines like the closing stanza of Chatterton's
poem 'The Resignation':

  The gloomy mantle of the night
    Which on my sinking spirit steals
  Will vanish at the morning light
    Which God, my East, my Sun reveals—

which justified Wordsworth in coupling him with Burns and calling Chatterton 'the marvellous boy'—'the sleepless soul that perished in his pride'.

Thinking it all over, I should call pride—energetic pride—the chief mark of Chatterton's poetry. And pride is the mark of really high poetry—of poetry in a phrase of William Blake's, who was one of Chatterton's admirers—which 'exists and exults in immortal thoughts'.

Think of some of the poets of pride—Shakespeare, Marlowe, Sir Walter Ralegh, Dryden, Pope, Landor, John Clare—it is their company Chatterton belongs to. Of course, Chatterton's poetry, Chatterton's pride, is incomplete—since he was seventeen when he killed himself. He only began:

> I thought of Chatterton, the marvellous boy,
> The sleepless soul that perished in his pride;
> Of him who walked in glory and in joy
> Following his plough along the mountain side:
> By our own spirits are we deified:
> We Poets in our youth begin in gladness;
> But thereof come in the end despondency and madness.

The end which comes to poets of pride, came much too quickly to Chatterton; we only have the beginning in gladness. But I do not think any other English poet—so far as we know—began with powers more remarkable: and that is why Chatterton, with his macaws and tigers and ruins and snakes, is there to be read; and not just remembered as a romantic boy who killed himself.

West of England, 1946